Inside
the Organization

Perspectives on
Employee Communications

Jack LeMenager

Fells Publishing, Third Edition, First Printing February 2017
Copyright © 2011, 2014, 2017 by Jack LeMenager

Address all inquiries to: Fells Publishing,
10 Johnson Road, Winchester, MA 01890.

Printed in the United States of America

ISBN: 978-1460940693

Title: Inside the Organization:
Perspectives on Employee Communications
by Jack LeMenager

1. Employee communications
2. Business communications
3. Leadership communications
4. Employee engagement
5. Change management

Cover Design by John G. Leonard
The Granville Group
Grass Valley, CA

Cover illustration: iStock.com

Table of Contents

Forward

When the essays comprising this book were written, we were reeling in an economic downturn seemingly without end, brought on by related banking, mortgage and financial missteps and ills.

In that period, from 2008 to 2011, the challenges facing businesses were multi-layered and complex. Lay-offs or the threat of them hovered over many if not most companies, to say nothing of the possibility of business failure. Managers and employees were feeling insecure, justifiably, while company leaders sought ways to get ahead of the crisis to survive and, ultimately, thrive.

Consequently, the thrust and main theme of many of these essays written then centered on the fall-out from such a stressful business environment, offering counsel to leaders, managers, communicators and employees for managing through tough times.

While many would argue those days are behind us, and our economy has mostly recovered, the lessons we learned then that I've tried to encapsulate in these essays continue to be relevant. Just because your business is showing a healthy profit now and you are able to expand and hire new employees does not mean the rules of the game have been suspended. If businesses are to succeed in the long-term, managers and business leaders still must engage their employees as though they are enduring tough times.

With a nod to the intervening years, I've refreshed these essays, added new anecdotes and examples, and made other edits to freshen the writing and messages. I trust you will appreciate the insights and lessons as much now as you might have six years ago.

Jack LeMenager
May 2017

Communities of Humans

"The community stagnates without the impulse of the individual.
The impulse dies away without the sympathy of the community."

William James
Philosopher
1842 – 1910

The Job Is More Than a Paycheck

"Companies die because their managers focus on the economic activity of producing goods and services, and they forget that their organizations' true nature is that of a community of humans."

A client shared that quote with me. I think it's one of the best summations of the chief reason for consistent, timely, and relevant employee engagement and communications that build trust and strong, lasting relationships within an organization, within each unique community of humans that is a business.

The quote was attributed to Arie de Geus, former head of Global Planning for Royal Dutch Shell, now retired, he was also a fellow at London School of Economics and Massachusetts Institute of Technology. He authored the book, "The Living Company."

I got to thinking about those words and their sentiment when, in February 2009, I learned that *The Rocky Mountain News* was shutting down. I had once done consulting work for its parent organization and knew a number of people associated with the paper. I wasn't surprised by the inevitable news but, naturally, I felt badly about it and wanted to learn the details. So I visited its web site, which featured a twenty-minute video that, at its heart, I sensed, reinforced de Geus' words.

The newspaper closed less than two months shy of the 150th anniversary of its founding. That's a lot of history for any organization, especially one that chronicled that history. In fact, the founding of the newspaper predates Colorado statehood by seventeen years. You can imagine the kinds of news it covered over the years: the settling of the American West, silver and gold prospecting in the Rocky Mountains west of Denver, claim jumpers, gunfights, and everything since.

The staff knew the end was near because *The News'* owner, Scripps-Howard, announced in January that it was seeking a buyer and that, if none stepped forward within a month, it would close the operation.

The newspaper business in general had been struggling for some time, having lost advertising revenue and readers to the Internet. But combining that fact with a dour economic climate at the time and *The News'* fate was sealed.

The interim period gave the people the opportunity to prepare the paper's obituary, so to speak, including the expertly produced and poignant video, as well as a fifty-two-page history of the newspaper inserted into its final edition.

But it was the video that touched me and evoked de Gaus' words. Staff reporters and editors were interviewed, and the viewer sensed the tears about to flow. It was a sad wake, as though they had lost a parent too soon. In fact, it may even have been more profound and sadder than that.

These people lost not only a job; they lost a mission they shared with dozens of other people within an entity called *The Rocky Mountain News* with which they all identified deeply, an almost living being that they helped shape and define every day, whose history they continued to help shape.

Those were tough times for a lot of businesses. Hundreds of thousands of people were losing their jobs. That video made the effect real. It conveyed a deeper understanding of what losing a job means.

We commit the majority of our waking hours throughout our adult lives to our jobs and careers. We define ourselves and sustain a significant sense of our self-worth and value from what we are able to achieve, each in our own way, on the job. Take that away from us, and what are we left with?

This is the core question that people ask themselves as they contemplate the potential loss of their own jobs in economic downturns, as they watch colleagues escorted out the door by company security guards, their personal effects shoved into a copier paper box. Sure, the lost paycheck is the big immediate concern. "How will I pay the mortgage? How will I cover the bills? What about my family? Will I be able to find a new job?"

But the deeper pain and self-doubt arises from the disconnection from that "community of humans" that was the organization we worked for, that community that defined us and from which we derived so much sense of identity, satisfaction, and our connection to the larger world; that organization we helped shape and define, which in turn shaped and defined us.

Rather than seeing people as numbers on a spreadsheet, managers and company leadership must think about this aspect of people's jobs and lives as they contemplate cutbacks, layoffs and the like. They must continually engage their people to build trust and understanding, especially in difficult times, as they contemplate the extreme measures they might have to take to account for fewer customers, to counter-balance slumping revenues and profits. They must convey an honest empathy with their people and a sincere faith in the value and contributions those people bring to the greater whole that the company represents.

That's what Arie de Gaus' words are all about. Managers must focus their thinking on the reality of their organization as a community of humans first and foremost. If they always do that – if they have always done that – chances are that the fruitful and profitable economic activity of producing goods and services will follow.

Who knows? Perhaps the bite of an economic downturn will have less effect on their "community of humans" and enable the organization to weather the temporary storms and live to see better days.

Look For Help in the Right Places

The field house was hot and stuffy that Sunday afternoon in late August as the incoming freshmen and their families gathered inside. The new students were to be officially welcomed by the university president. It had been a long and tiring day for our son as we helped him move into his dormitory room. Unfortunately (though understandably), he nodded off during the most helpful part of the president's address.

"I have nine words of advice for each new class," the president said as our son snoozed. *"Go to class. Do the work. Ask for help."*

The last three words, he explained, were the most critical in assuring the students' success in their coming four years at the university and were emblematic of the institution's team-based approach to higher education. He added that they shouldn't think less of themselves for needing help. Then he told an anecdote to illustrate his point.

After the president had shared those same words of counsel with a new member of the university's board of trustees to give him insights into the university and its approach, the new trustee in turn shared his own version of *Ask for help.*

He had founded two successful companies and had always believed in asking for help, no matter its source. In one particularly difficult challenge, he recalled, his company was working with a client when he recognized that the most talented person working on the project was an employee of the client company. Rather than struggle on, he requested the temporary reassignment of this skilled person to his team "to be sure we delivered the highest quality solution." He saw nothing wrong in asking for help. In fact, he saw it as a requirement of the job.

His anecdote intrigued this parent. Such counsel contradicts the *"Not Invented Here"* attitude, an approach that says that, if you're the outside expert, your solution is always going to be best, regardless, and to reach out to others for help is a sign of weakness.

I've never believed that and I loathe working with people who do. In a similar vein, I have occasionally found that a client's approach works well. Why fix what isn't broken? In those cases, my counsel, after examining the situation closely, is usually that they continue in that manner, though I may suggest a modification or two, as well as an appropriate follow-on methodology (which is often missing).

Managers and outside counselors should be honest enough to know when their solution is no better than another approach. Or, like the trustee's story, they should recognize when someone else is better equipped to help drive the team toward the highest quality solution, and then seek their help.

We see this at play both within internal teams and when outsiders are brought in. In an internal environment, this can play out in a number of ways, both good and bad.

Petty jealousies among peers can lead to a situation where, in pursuit of greater reward and recognition, the stronger-willed person downplays, denigrates, or nit-picks a teammate's more elegant, simpler, or more practical solution.

Sometimes, a manager wants to take credit for solving a problem, casting him/herself as the most talented and experienced person on the project, perhaps ignoring an employee's better solution or that person's superior talent.

The late great sportswriter Red Smith remembered his days at the old (and now defunct) *New York Herald-Tribune*. Sports editor Stanley Woodward returned from World War 2 and set about building what was then and probably remains the best collection of sportswriters ever assembled. "He was scouting for the best men he could get" in each field, Smith recalled. "Stanley was the best department head, perhaps the best all-around newspaperman I've ever known. Some sports editors, especially if they write a column, are afraid of competition. They want to be the big man of the paper. But Stanley's rule was, 'I don't want anyone who can't out-write me'."

Those are sound words of advice, whether applied directly in regard to a manager's relationship with his/her direct reports or in the case of the outsider. The important thing is the end goal. We should all be seeking the best possible solution, no matter the source, to the challenge at hand so that we can achieve the organization's business objectives.

Mature people, whether in business or in school, should take to heart this counsel upon which the university president elaborated as several hundred students began their university educations.

Recognize when you need help. Don't be so proud that you won't or can't ask for it. Know whom to turn to. And when you get that help, take advantage of it. (And don't forget to say "thank you.")

By the way, we let our son know the sage advice he'd missed. My wife wrote it on an index card and pinned it to his bulletin board. When he struggles, we remind him to ask for help.

How to Lose An Employee's Loyalty

A college buddy, Walt, had worked for the same Portland, OR-based company since our graduation. The 85-year-old family-owned manufacturer had always treated its employees well. Walt worked his way up through the ranks on merit, dedication, and hard work.

A few years ago, Walt was promoted to be among the company's top six executives, reporting to the CEO, who admired his loyalty and knack for keeping key customers happy. But soon, everything would change.

A year later, a German company, a competitor in the European market, made an offer to the family owners that proved irresistible. The grandchildren of the late founder would become spectacularly wealthy overnight. The third generation had never been directly involved in the business, so their decision to sell was easy.

When I talked to him after he had visited the German headquarters of the new owners, Walt was encouraged. He was led to believe that there might be opportunities for further promotion within the parent organization, a holding company with subsidiaries in related businesses. It might even mean a transfer to Europe, which intrigued him. There was also a lot of talk about reinvesting in the newly acquired American operation, taking it to a new level of excellence, he said.

Three years later, Walt had left for a better job with the chief competitor, something he had never before contemplated. In fact, he thought he would retire from this company. What changed?

Six months after the acquisition, the CEO who had overseen the phenomenal growth of the previous twenty years was unceremoniously let go. The new owners inserted their own man, a German national, to run the North American operation. That's when everything started changing, for the worst, according to Walt.

The firm's largest customer was headquartered outside Atlanta, with manufacturing, assembly and distribution facilities scattered around North America. Walt had developed strong relationships with the key people there over the years, traveling cross-country frequently to meet them, as well as visiting their several plants around the continent to troubleshoot problems.

Like most of the firm's customers, Walt serviced this client well, solving its problems quickly through his close attention to details and first-hand awareness of how they used his company's products.

He knew how critical quality and on-time delivery were to this customer. His years of working at the company in various capacities gave him insight into how to unblock bottlenecks and get things done on behalf of customers. It was an approach replicated with the company's many other customers with whom Walt dealt.

The changes at Walt's company came slowly at first. He had previously been given a lot of leeway in how he operated, how he took care of the company's most important customers, such as jumping on a plane on a moment's notice to visit a customer's plant. Now, all his big and little decisions were being second-guessed by the new CEO's assistants. What had once been fun and simple became unnecessarily complicated.

Low-level finance department people in Germany, who didn't know Walt and were nearly young enough to be his children, were scrutinizing his expense reports as never before. His spur-of-the-moment travels to meet with clients were cut back in the interest of saving money. Airline tickets had to be purchased in advance for fare breaks. Cost cutting also negatively affected product quality and order fulfillment. Walt started getting a lot more complaints from customers. Parts did not meet specifications. On-time delivery requirements were not being met. Soon, his best customers were bringing in second supply sources. Since his travel allowance had been cut, he was unable to visit to address customer concerns personally.

So when his firm's top competitor came knocking, Walt was receptive. They soon made him a generous offer, and he accepted without a second thought. He joined them with comparable responsibilities, along with better remuneration, perks, and incentives.

The day he left, he walked into the CEO's office, submitted his resignation and left. The boss wasn't interested enough even to ask why.

But the question remained, why would a senior level person, who had been with the company more than twenty years, suddenly leave? His departure echoed across the organization. Departure of a well-known and popular manager meant that everyone's worst fears about the new owners were being realized. If Walt would leave, it's bad, they must have thought.

When gifted and talented people like Walt leave their long-time employers, their move is indicative of significant internal change that an organization's most valuable employees cannot tolerate. Talented contributors stay committed to their companies when they are given reason to be loyal, not only in how they are rewarded but also in the respect and support they get in their jobs and the pride their companies instill in them.

11

Take that away and you have taken away the reason for their loyalty and commitment. It becomes just another job, interchangeable with any other job with a comparable paycheck.

The irony in such situations is that these companies lose the people they can least afford to, their most talented contributors, while the guys who keep their heads down, don't take risks, and don't contribute a lot to the betterment of the organization stay on.

Organizations must establish, then follow their mission to carry them and their people through times of challenge and difficult change, whether it's an acquisition, management shake-up, or brutal market forces.

In the case of Walt's company, its mission had been an unrelenting dedication to meeting customers' needs by delivering top-notch quality and providing responsive service. When the new owners took over, though they likely never would have said so openly, their core mission was profitability through cost cutting. It was their actions, not their words, that demonstrated their true mission of profitability.

I've seen contradictory missions like that elsewhere. For instance, a newly acquired company known for its entrepreneurial spirit and drive became consumed and overwhelmed by its new parent's obsession with policies, processes, and procedures. The true entrepreneurs at the operational levels in the acquired company were stifled, soon frustrated, and then out the door within a year.

Acquiring companies may and often do speak to the concerns of their new employees coming to them through the acquisition. "Of course! Yes!" they may say. "We believe in an entrepreneurial approach to business, just like you." But when actions contradict the words, the truth is out.

Walt was similarly excited about the words he heard from his company's new owner, words about re-investing in the business to make it better at what it already did so well. But the ultimate actions of cost cutting bore out the truth. And the true nature of its future direction is something he chose not to be associated with. It was truly their loss.

An Easy Way to Motivate People

Given the chance to boost employee morale, to reinforce the kind of messages and behaviors that help build a cohesive organization, what kind of company would pass it up? It's hard to imagine that any organization wouldn't want to maximize every opportunity to make people feel a part of something larger than themselves. So it struck me as absolutely tone-deaf and obtuse when I observed a company that missed just such an opportunity.

Escorted into the lobby of the headquarters of a multi-national corporation, at the time a potential client, I was heartened to see a wall of larger-than-life black-and-white photographic portraits of people: clerical employees, blue-collar factory workers, and executives in various poses related to the work they do.

I recognized the CEO and a couple members of his senior management team in the photos and commented aloud to my companion, the prospective client liaison, what a great idea it is to post all those employee photos in the lobby. It reinforced the sense of community that helps define a corporation and its mission, I said.

I imagined myself as an employee coming into work every morning, feeling a sense of pride at seeing the photo of myself alongside my fellow employees. "What a terrific idea," I said, "putting up all those photos of the workforce like that."

So imagine my shock and surprise when she said that all but the handful of senior executives portrayed there were, in fact, models and not actual employees of the company.

14

Talk about a missed opportunity. Talk about a self-inflicted (and fatal) wound. Ouch!

Not only would a wall of employee photos have been a real morale booster and enhance people's pride in and connection to the organization, but the company's failure to do so, and in such a brusque, blatant fashion, had the complete opposite effect. Were I an employee there, the knowledge and daily reminder of seeing a wall of photos of paid models pretending to be real employees would be a daily slap in the face. It would tell me that employees are replaceable by anonymous models and therefore not essential to the organization or its mission and therefore interchangable.

What possibly could have been the motivation? Cost saving? Was it honestly cheaper to hire dozens of models and take professional photos? Not likely.

In the delicate dance typical of conversations with a prospective client, I handled the topic gingerly. Fortunately, she agreed with me and, in fact, said that she felt insulted just as I would have been had I worked there.

The experience revealed volumes about this organization and the people who ran it. But it also spoke to the broader issue of engaging employees in the organization and its mission.

Businesses are, at their heart, communities of humans. Anything that enhances the cohesiveness of that community, that builds people's sense of connection to the greater whole, is going to accrue to the benefit of the corporation.

Connecting employees to the corporation can take many forms, and the more methods employed, the better. Frequent face-to-face meetings with senior level people, executive visibility and availability, communications in numerous venues and such all add up to a better-informed and better-connected employee population, employees who are engaged in the long and short -term goals of the organization.

Envision a company that does all that and then imagine how well a wall of employee photos would be received, and how natural the addition of such photos would be. Now, consider the opposite.

Without revealing the name of the company, I can assure you that it wound up in dire financial straits. Five years after my having seen those photos in the lobby, the company filed for bankruptcy. In my own mind, I see a causal connection between that bankruptcy and that wall of photos. Sadly, it was a missed opportunity.

Keep Employees Connected After the Merger

In early 2009, Oracle was on a buying spree, taking advantage of a weak economy to pick up a few bargains. It was akin to what most people would do in terms of upgrading their housing situation in those circumstances, if only they had had the cash on hand to do it.

At the time, Oracle did have a lot of cash on hand – about $7.4 billion, to be precise. So CEO Larry Ellison went shopping, beefing up his company's product and service offerings by paying cash and stock to buy ten different companies in the previous twelve months. It was about a year later that Oracle made its biggest acquisition ever, Sun Microsystems.

While safeguarding its future bottom line with a broader selection of products and services, the company's near-term challenges were happening off Ellison's radar screen – the actual integration of these often disparate companies and cultures into the behemoth that Oracle had become. A telling comment by one employee, quoted in *The Wall Street Journal* (February 17, 2009), pointed out the crux of this problem:

> *"Some former employees . . . say the acquisitions spawned confusion in-house as people got thrown together on new projects. 'My manager would put me on projects that are totally irrelevant for my skill set,' said one former consultant who joined Oracle when it bought PeopleSoft Inc. in 2004. The changes became so frequent, he says, he eventually stopped trying to remember the names of groups he was assigned to."*

17

Merging one company into another is a long-term and often difficult process, all the more difficult when the acquired company is large, with a lot of employees in a variety of operations, located in numerous places around the world.

The big numbers guys, people like Larry Ellison and his peers, can confidently seal the deal and head off looking for the next acquisition that makes sense. In their wake, they leave a lot of people who have to make the latest deal work, sewing together the mismatched seams that occur at the many points of contact.

At its heart, the integration of two companies is all about hundreds of small but important tasks, the dotting of i's and crossing of t's, that consume thousands of man-hours in bringing together two different organizations to assure that the original value and intent of the acquisition are realized.

Integrations aren't completed when the deal closes. That's just the starting point. Typically, as many as one, two or even three years later, there may still be loose ends. Individuals at some foreign operations might nonetheless be operating under "temporary" contracts and not officially part of their new company. I've seen cases where local labor laws, especially in the nations comprising the European Union (EU), prevent the new company from even issuing new business cards until all labor laws have been satisfied to enable these people to become official employees of the acquiring company.

The HR people, meanwhile, tear their hair out over these kinds of complications, trying to sort out the nuances and keep everyone happy and productive. The IT operation is still another matter. Among other tasks, the IT folks have to align two networks to ensure that people on both sides of the integration can readily communicate and securely share critical, sensitive information. Even in a software company like Oracle, it likely takes months before employees in the acquired firms have full access to internal web sites, file sharing software, and assorted applications.

And then there's the personal angle. Noses get out of joint when people in the acquired company lose the cherished titles they had earned over years of dedicated service and hard work in their formerly independent firm. Maybe a "senior vice president" at XYZ Software is now a "director" at Oracle, one of hundreds with that title. Sure, his salary and benefits stayed the same, but when he moved onto Oracle's campus, he lost his corner office, reserved parking space, and other perks and the respect that went with being an SVP at the smaller firm. Ruffled feathers like that need to be smoothed, lest the valuable birds fly away.

Meanwhile, business can't stand still while details around payroll, benefits, IT access, and job titles are sorted out. People on both sides of the integration are expected to be working together from Day One, creating, designing, producing, selling, and servicing products, keeping customers happy, and finding new customers.

In all this, communication plays an important role. The temptation is to fly at the twenty-thousand-foot level, looking for the common cultural links that help one group better understand and merge with the other. Narratives distill the essence of the acquisition strategy that brought them together and can then be used to help shape internal messages and reinforce the core themes. That's an important part of the process.

But the most valuable communications are those that establish broad internal awareness and understanding of the challenges everyone is facing, while providing timelines to give people a sense that there is reason for optimism; communications that anticipate and answer people's burning questions, the open issues that keep them awake at night. That's what matters most.

The Value of Saying *"Thank You"*

Our parents taught us always to use the magic words, "please" and "thank you." They often couched the suggestion with various aphorisms like, "You catch more flies with honey than you do with vinegar."

Tired and trite as such counsel may seem, the core truth is timeless and unchanged. Such behavior is important, especially in a business setting. Further, a manager's "please" and "thank you" carry much more meaning to employees than they do coming from a peer. That's because people appreciate recognition, especially when it comes from those who may have the capacity to shape their future.

In the course of interviewing employees in a client company a few years ago, we heard a story from people in one of its unionized paper mills that underlines this point.

Late in the afternoon one day, a critical component machine broke down, causing a shutdown of the entire paper machine, a massive and complex system that produces tremendous volumes of paper round-the-clock, every day. An early diagnosis determined it would keep the line down for at least forty-eight hours, maybe longer. The maintenance team, consisting of about a half-dozen men, dove in, and stayed past quitting time. In fact, they worked through the night and, by mid-morning the next day, had the machine up and running again. The projected forty-eight hours of downtime was cut to a mere fifteen, potentially saving the company tens of thousands of dollars in lost production.

Sure, these union machinists were on the clock. And, of course, they collected a hefty overtime bonus for their hard work. And while the union contract allowed them to quit after their requisite eight hours and return the next day at their usual starting time, as a team, they decided to work through the night and get the paper machine back up and running.

A couple days later, after these men punched in one morning, their supervisor greeted them with a boxful of fresh donuts, a pot of hot coffee, a "thank you" for each, and a big smile. He paid for the coffee and donuts out of his own pocket. The smile and "thank you's" were free.

Seems like a simple gesture and an obvious one.

When one of these guys on the team told us the story, he got emotional and a little choked up at the recollection. In fact, when I retell the story, so do I.

Before we finished our project there, we heard that same story a total of four times from different people, only one of whom was a member of the original crew who had worked through the night. The story was so compelling that everyone we talked to seemed familiar with it. Now, here's the amazing part.

We later learned that the actual event had taken place more than three years before we heard about it. Small effort? Yes. Big impact? You bet.

When businesspeople talk about "reward and recognition," it usually is in terms of formal systems, where people's performance is measured on the fiscal year and they earn credit toward a reward, a gift card, extra time off, or something from the company store.

Maybe they get their name in the company newsletter or a dinner out with their spouse at a fancy local restaurant. That's all well and good, and I don't disparage or discourage that kind of activity.

But if that is the only way people are recognized for their hard work and commitment, the result will be a closely aligned set of behaviors within the margins of those pre-set determinants of desirable conduct.

Go ahead and do that, if you wish, but don't overlook the far more important and meaningful kinds of reward and recognition, the simple ones, like:

- A big smile
- A pat on the back
- A *"Thank you for your hard work"*
- Impromptu team meetings to tell them that they're doing a heckuva good job

In short, say the kinds of things you yourself would want to hear from your manager. You'll be amazed at how well your words are received. Who knows? Maybe they'll talk about it for years to come.

Manage People's Expectations in an Acquisition

The firm is opening a Los Angeles office, one young copywriter speculates aloud. "I'd love to move to LA. Get myself a convertible," he says. No one knows for sure what is happening to their New York advertising agency, Sterling Cooper. But something surely is afoot, as the partners remain huddled behind closed doors in the executive conference room throughout the morning.

It turns out the firm is being acquired by a larger London ad agency. "There's definitely going to be some redundancies," says a secretary once the news leaks. Everyone is panicked. Is their job going to be deemed "redundant?"

An account manager lowers his voice conspiratorially. "Regime change is always tricky. You want to stay neutral. Loyalists are always hung, and you don't want to get caught in the fall-out."

Another adds, "They don't care about us. We're just a bunch of salaries on a ledger. They'll draw a line and get rid of everything below it." The traffic manager whines, "I like this company the way it is."

Sound familiar? Is it real life? No, but it may as well be. It was a scene from the final episode of the second season of *Mad Men*, an original dramatic series on cable TV from AMC. Placed in the early 1960s, the episode no doubt accurately reflects the gut fear that is felt among employees in a company about to be acquired.

For dramatic effect, while the news of the merger was sifting through the Sterling Cooper organization, there was a tangible fear overhanging the world due to the October 1962 Cuban missile crisis, which mirrors and exacerbates the fear and angst felt by those in the firm and their uncertainties about the coming merger and the future.

This isn't 1962 and times do change, but not in the realm of mergers and acquisitions and their effect on the people at ground level, those who will not reap the big financial windfalls that owners and partners do.

Mergers and acquisitions foment uncertainty, dislocation and fear – and worse. The natural human reaction to radical change like that cannot be avoided. Changes brought on by such events as acquisitions and mergers also spawn questions that cannot be answered right away. And when questions can't be answered promptly, the rumor mill takes over.

What *can* be managed, on the other hand, are people's expectations. They can also be given insights into how decisions affecting their lives will be made, and when, as well as information as to why some questions will remain open for a time.

In today's business world, much of the value of an acquired firm resides in its people. The acquiring company buys brand names, patents, manufacturing facilities, equipment, and the like, to be sure. But without the people, it's an empty shell. So it's incumbent on the senior managers to do all within their power to reassure the people and reinforce the company's core values so that the top talent won't make a beeline for the door the day the sale closes.

This is particularly true in a people-intensive business like advertising. Legendary ad agency founder David Ogilvy used to say that his equity went down the elevators every night. He was right. It was and still is a fact of that business. But it's also true in all other businesses as well, even those that are capital-intensive, such as manufacturers.

At base, effective, relevant, and timely communications will go far in achieving the core business purpose of the merger, which is to preserve and enhance the value of the acquired company by building trust and credibility among the newly added employees.

Often, the danger lies in the early days before much is known and few of the big questions can be answered due to the necessary secrecy that surrounds such transactions. The acquiring firm will often communicate reassuring words that "nothing (or little) will change" and that people should just keep doing what they've always done.

But as the deal is completed and the questions begin to find answers, the early general communications may be inadvertently contradicted. It can't be helped. Much is discovered in the early "honeymoon" phase that hadn't been or couldn't have been anticipated, necessitating unplanned changes in plans.

Communications should avoid assumptions and blanket public statements in the early days of a merger or acquisition. Kraft Foods CEO Irene Rosenfeld learned that lesson the hard way. Shortly after Kraft's March 2010 acquisition of Cadbury's, she promised that a plant in Britain, which Cadbury's had scheduled for shutdown prior to its acquisition by Kraft, would not be closed after all.

Unfortunately, she learned within months of the deal's closing that she and her team hadn't fully understood the situation and so couldn't keep that promise. She took a lot of heat for her miscalculation, which whipsawed hundreds of people, who thought their lost jobs had been saved, but in the end hadn't.

It also became a hot political issue because the country was in the midst of a national election and the topic became a political football that the sitting (and soon to be ousted) Labour government of Gordon Brown had to defend.

Change is like that. The key is to approach the employees and managers of the acquired firm with honesty and reassurance. The core messages must stay simple, direct and honest:

- *We acquired your company because of the excellence it adds to ours. It would be unwise for us to do anything that diminishes or destroys its value or that excellence.*

- *Please work with us as we get to know one another better, as we learn how we will operate together going forward.*

- *Share with us your best practices and show us how they might benefit the new larger company.*

- *Please understand that there will be stumbles along the way. We will always try to minimize the mistakes and hope that you will stick with us through the rough patches.*

- *By working together, by striving to achieve the best for our customers, our employees, and our stockholders, we will all succeed together, and the final product will be more than the sum of the two components.*

Re-engage Employees After the Layoffs

Few businesspeople alive today have ever faced such a prolonged economic slump as in the years following the 2008 financial crash, nor the multitude of challenges it generated. This was new territory for almost everyone. How well people operated going forward determined the speed at which they, both individually and collectively, pulled out of this economic sluggishness.

While in the midst of that downturn, I could confidently say that "this too shall pass" and we would eventually see an expanding economy with renewed job growth. But I am no economist and certainly had no crystal ball to foresee when that turn-around would come or how.

But I can opine on internal business environments and how leaders, managers, and their employees should be operating together to serve the best interests of their companies and help assure their survival through rough times.

Regardless of which way the economy goes, leaders' and managers' uppermost focus must always remain on the perpetuation and long-term success of the company, a goal that encompasses many aspects of running a business and making countless decisions, big and small. But if business leaders and managers do only one thing right in these trying times, it has to be treating their employees with respect.

When the economy started slowing and sinking in 2008, many companies had to impose layoffs. And even if they hadn't laid anyone off, virtually all companies, even those with strong balance sheets, continued to consider or enact pre-emptive budget cuts, including wage and hiring freezes. The result? Nervous and insecure employees everywhere.

Clearly, employees are not likely to do their best work in that state of mind, which is the last thing an already stressed organization needs. Nor is anyone likely to take the kind of informed risks that help companies innovate and break away from the competitive pack.

Businesses need their people to be at their best to collectively surmount today's complex challenges. They can't afford to have disaffected or disconnected employees.

It's important, then, for managers and leaders to take some simple actions to counteract the unavoidable poisonous climate of fear that can set in and afflict even the best businesses under the cloud of budget cuts or a recent or potential layoff.

Downsizing and economic uncertainty is a time for dialogue based on facts and the realities of the marketplace. Words alone will not calm people's insecurities or fears. But the right behaviors and actions will. One valuable behavior is encouraging dialogue. Set up a system to invite feedback. Don't let anything fester. Keep the dialogue open. And then listen mindfully.

Re-engage the workforce in the business at hand by restating business goals and the strategies that will get you there. Remind them in succinct terms why you're in business. Bring the outside world in to re-emphasize the climate of uncertainty within which the company is operating, including the challenges your customers, suppliers, and competitors may be facing.

Acknowledge people's frustrations, uncertainties, and insecurities. But, at the same time, remind them that this is the world we're all operating in today. The only thing they can control is what they do every day and how well they do it.

Re-iterate what is important (the business goals) and make sure that they see their connection to and responsibility in fulfilling those goals. Employees have a significant role to play in this dynamic. In addition to their willingness and desire to put in the extra effort, they should be open to new ideas and new ways of doing things. They should also be encouraged to bring new ideas forward.

The need for honesty is also critical, alerting their supervisors and managers to new opportunities and unanticipated problems, along with proposed solutions. Employees should also remain curious about the world outside their company, especially customers, but also the global economic climate and the many facets of the world that have direct and indirect impacts on how the company operates.

Leadership needs to keep managers in the loop so there is a common understanding of the marketplace realities that led to the action (e.g., layoffs and/or budget cuts), the company's business strategy going forward, and the employees' roles and responsibilities to drive toward those goals.

Prepare backgrounder documents for the managers to ensure that employees across the organization are hearing a consistent message, and that managers are prepared to answer the tough questions they will inevitably field.

There's an unspoken truth when people are laid off—their work still must get done. But where is that work going? How is that particular operation, function, or department going to make up for the lost manpower and productivity?

Who is going to take on that burden? What work or project needs to be stopped, delayed, postponed, or reassigned? These are often the first and most difficult questions on everyone's mind after the dust of downsizing settles.

Be prepared with realistic, workable answers. Be sure that your managers and supervisors are conscious of the need to help people prioritize their many tasks within the scope of the business' many challenges and opportunities.

In their New Year's January 12, 2009, *Business Week* column, Jack and Suzy Welch offered another valuable piece of timeless advice:

> *". . . resist the impulse to make 2009 a year devoid of celebration. When times get tough, leaders often assume it's unseemly to stop now and again and, well, have some fun. But this year, because of its severe challenges, is sure to be filled with remarkable small victories and heroic efforts. What a lost opportunity to build morale it would be, then, not to recognize and reward the people who are over-delivering. More than ever, they need and deserve it."*

If we learned anything from those frightful, uncertain times, let's hope it was the central importance of showing respect for employees by communicating with them frequently, openly, and honestly, and reminding ourselves why we're doing this, our company's core driving purpose. That's a truth that applies not just in bad times, but in good times as well.

Effective Employee Communications

*"The most important thing in communication
is hearing what isn't said."*

Peter Drucker
Author, Management Consultant
1909 - 2005

There is No Such Thing as a Boilerplate Communications Plan

An online discussion group about employee communications elicited the following panicked, clearly last-minute call for help: *"Does anyone have a good internal communication plan they'd be willing to share?"*

The notion that there is such a thing as a one-size-fits-all approach to communication planning is absurd on its face. Using a boilerplate communications plan is like shopping for shoes when you're in training for a marathon. Without specificity, you could wind up with ski boots, which are shoes, but certainly won't suit the needs of a long distance runner.

In the same sense, in communications planning, no two situations are alike. Think of the multitude of possibilities. Are we talking about a financial institution or a manufacturer of machine tools? Is our target audience unionized employees in a single factory or field salespeople working on commission spread across a continent selling electronic components? Are we trying to communicate with mid-level managers at an international medical device company or non-commissioned U.S. Army officers based outside the country? I'm sure you get the idea.

The point of any communications plan is to ensure that the *right information* gets to the *right people* at the *right time* through means that reach them most effectively, and that that information is relevant to them and actionable.

There is a practical way to begin to develop an appropriate

communications plan for any given set of circumstances, without resorting to a boilerplate plan (if you could even find one). But it requires a lot of homework, along with a lot of serious thought and analysis. The initial steps and their basic questions are always the same, regardless of the circumstances.

- Who is your audience? Define it both specifically and generally in ways that mean something to you and your management team, such as those variables cited above.
- Know as much as possible about your target audience, especially how they prefer to get information and what they consider their most (and least) credible information sources.
- Determine what you want them to know *and why*.
- What do you want them to do as a result of getting your communication? *Why?* After they do that, then what?
- Is there any time sensitivity in the communication?

If you can't answer *all* these simple questions, then you have no reason to communicate. Answering these questions will put you in a better position to develop an appropriate and effective communications plan consisting of *what* (content), *how* (through what vehicles), *when* (timing and cadence) and, specifically, *to whom*.

The default approach should always be face-to-face communications with immediate supervisors where credibility is usually highest, where there is less chance of misunderstanding or misinterpretation, and where there is the best opportunity for timely dialogue and question-and-answer. Everything else you may do (e.g., newsletter, email, Twitter, blogs, Intranet postings, bulletin boards, posters, coffee mugs, etc.) should come later to reinforce and supplement what was already communicated directly by supervisors.

Your first communication, then, would be to the supervisors themselves, face-to-face with their managers, to ensure that they are fully informed and on board, with no doubts or misunderstandings. Also, the supervisors must know what the communication to employees is trying to achieve, what the employees need to know, why they need to know it, and what the employees are expected to do as a result of getting the information (the "action" component).

Avoid the path of least resistance (i.e., the easy route), a trap that many fall into. Don't rely on impersonal vehicles like emails as the first and/or only source of communication. Focus instead on achieving supervisor understanding and buy-in first so that they will be confident in conveying the necessary information to their direct reports, able to field both pertinent and extraneous questions.

Also, prepare those supervisors with questions they may likely get, along with the appropriate answers. Supervisors should also understand that, if they field questions they can't answer, they should promise to get the answer, and then follow through.

I hope that's what the online inquirer was looking for. But by the tone of his question, I think he wanted a shortcut and, when the boilerplate plan he was looking for wasn't forthcoming, he probably just fired off a bunch of emails to his target audience with his fingers crossed, hoping for the best.

That would have been a shame because, really, the answer to his question is pretty straightforward. The key to successful communications is understanding your audience and what you want them to do with the information you give them. It's that simple.

"Employee Communications" Is Not a Newsletter

At one time or another, you've undoubtedly found yourself having to explain what you do for a living to someone completely unfamiliar with your discipline. If your field is employee communications, as mine is, and someone at, say, a neighborhood Christmas party asks, you're eager to slip into your rote thirty-second elevator speech (if you have one) before he can say, "Oh, employee communications. I know all about that. You write newsletters." To which, I cringe.

Sometimes, I'm tempted instead just to say that "I work for the government, but I can't talk about it," give a conspiratorial wink, walk away, and leave it at that. Better that than the alternative of explaining why employee communications does not equal employee newsletters to someone who won't care enough to understand the difference and will quickly lose interest in my refutation.

Amazingly, I ran into a variation of this absurdity once when invited to pitch for an assignment to help improve the internal communications of a locally headquartered company. The business employed nearly 10,000 people at several sites around the U.S. and Canada. The head of Human Resources had sought outside support for the employee communications team that reported to him.

His "team" consisted of two hard-working, dedicated, and intelligent (though junior-level) people. I quickly sensed they were overwhelmed and poorly directed, and that they were looking for shortcuts to get things done, "things" being that which they sensed their boss wanted done or what he told them to do.

With respect to communications, their types of shortcuts aren't always good things. I've seen companies grow too comfortable with their established modes of communicating. These tools might be decades old, part of the fabric of the organization, even after they've lost any meaning or value to their audience. Unfortunately, I got the impression that was the case here.

As I soon concluded, their desire to "improve internal communications" came down to wanting an outsider's fresh approach to improve their monthly employee newsletter: i.e., better-written and more interesting stories, and more appealing graphics. Roughly half of the employees were in plants and distribution centers and did not have access to computers. So the tried-and-true printed newsletter was how they learned about their company, if they were interested enough to read it. And that presented a series of questions:

- Had anyone determined whether in fact this tool was the most effective way of reaching the employee audience?
- Was it bringing employees the information they wanted and needed?
- What kind of information did they want and need?
- Were people reading the newsletter?
- Was it relevant to them?
- Was it opening employees' minds to new ideas and new ways of doing their jobs?
- Were they connecting its messages to where the company needed to go?
- What were they doing or expected to do with the information gleaned from its pages?
- Or were copies of the newsletter just filling mailroom trashcans?

As I began to pose those questions, I sensed eyes glazing over. The questions were not being well received, nor would I likely get cogent or informed answers.

When I asked for examples of other internal communications, I was shown a series of sporadic emails from the CEO and his management team on a range of minor and major topics. There was also an "interactive" online "CEO's Forum," its most recent entry more than two months old. The interactive component was not apparent to me. It was all one-way. An occasional "Letter from the CEO" appeared in the newsletter. The tone and content of the two were virtually the same.

One person told me that the CEO and/or members of his management team held infrequent "town hall meetings" to make important announcements, though she couldn't remember the last one or its core message. For that matter, she couldn't tell me the last time she had spoken to any of the senior people or seen them on site. (Incidentally, this site was a couple miles down the road from the building that housed company executives, not some distant city.)

The problem at this company and, no doubt, others today boils down to this: It has become too easy for leaders and managers to let technology, no matter how antiquated, do their communicating. In fact, executives are not communicating effectively when their communications are simply emails, newsletters, and online postings, where the medium becomes more important than the message. Media, no matter how sophisticated, do not engage employees in the business and its vision, even if it's blogging or tweeting.

When a company's definition and understanding of "employee communications" is a newsletter or email, or when information is expected to "cascade" down into the organization as if by magic, it's likely indicative of a deeper, more harmful problem.

It means that little consideration is being given to the real communications that should be occurring within and across the organization, the daily face-to-face exchanges of ideas, insights, and information between and among leaders, managers and employees; communications in which leadership engages the organization in the company's mission and vision.

When that's the case, when leadership is trying to take the company one way while the employees are going in the opposite direction because they're misinformed, ill-informed, or uninformed, the problems multiply and fester, resulting in poor financial results and weak long-term growth prospects.

Because the decision-maker in this case, the head of HR, seemed so set on fixing and improving the newsletter as the solution, without fully appreciating or even being interested in delving into the company's deeper issues and challenges, I took a pass on the opportunity.

This company's communications and employee engagement problems were far more severe than just fixing a boring newsletter. They were, in fact, far worse than its HR director knew or could have imagined. No sense beating my head against that wall.

Employee Understanding Requires an Ongoing Effort

Can employees be "educated" about the realities of the marketplace? It seems that among a lot of corporate leadership these days, there is a belief that "education" is the path by which employees will be helped to "see the light" as to what's going on outside the company, to help them put their internal reality into context.

The ultimate goal is appropriate and admirable. It's the implied attitude that's worrisome. The term "educate" troubles me. It suggests a point of view that sees employees as less worldly than they ought to be, at least less so than the managers who speak in those terms. Big mistake. It's an assumption that often betrays an environment where, until a crisis hits, management basically keeps the general employee population in the dark.

There often comes a time, a crisis point, where it's critical that the internal audience has a clear awareness and understanding of the external realities that are forcing radical changes on the organization. This innate awareness and understanding gives employees a firm foundation on which to operate. But if corporate leaders reach that crisis point and find themselves scrambling to bring the internal audience up to speed, it's too late. Reality bites back.

Let's go back to the ultimate goal, to raise awareness and understanding among employees about the realities of the business so they are better equipped to put their own work and responsibilities in the larger context and more likely to respond to a crisis in an appropriate and helpful manner.

Yes, employees need to have a full awareness and understanding of the external world and its many impacts on their organization and their livelihoods. But it's awareness and understanding that come with conscious engagement over time. It's not like a snow blower, brought out of the garage when the blizzard hits.

Awareness and understanding are achieved not through information and engagement in the midst of a crisis, but rather through on-going cultivation, through a deliberate effort to foster dialogue and discussion, even debate (when appropriate), inside the organization. This requires an attitude and accompanying behavior of openness and engagement that starts at the top of the organization.

If the CEO consistently engages her/his direct reports and other managers in open dialogue, discussion and debate about the challenges and opportunities facing the company, it's clear that that is an acceptable and appropriate behavior for the organization. Having been engaged in such a manner by their managers, middle managers in turn do so with their direct reports, and supervisors with theirs, and so on down the line. Employees learn that dialogue, discussion, and debate are valued, so the information flows both directions.

In this era of reduced manpower, where employees are increasingly asked to assume greater responsibility without adequate supervision and support, it's best that they have a firm foundation of understanding of how their manager thinks and why, so they can infer the right choices, should the need for a hasty decision arise.

That foundation is built over time, under the guidance and clear-headed thinking of a focused management team that not only knows the company's vision, but the route by which they will achieve that vision and how best to communicate it to the organization.

Communicating that vision is achieved through engagement:

discussion, dialogue, and debate. The successful organization brings into this discussion the world outside the company, around questions such as these:

- How is the economy affecting our customers?
- What has changed for them? What do our customers need and expect from us in this climate versus before?
- How are our competitors responding?
- Where can we anticipate the market to go next?
- Who might be our future competitors, companies that we don't now perceive as competitors? Why?
- How can we beat those future competitors before they get started? What aren't we doing or offering our customers that might be creating an opening to our market for newcomers?
- Where are we most vulnerable, in terms of product/service offerings, customer service/support, pricing, etc.?
- What are the potential markets for our products/services where we don't now compete?

These kinds of questions and the dialogue they stimulate are valuable on a number of levels, not the least of which is engaging employees in the business. Managers often learn more from their employees than the other way around. People in the trenches, as it were, can have unique insights that those in the C-Suite don't. Most important, though, this kind of dialogue engages employees in the real business of the company—its future.

Employees' stake in the game becomes obvious to them. Their commitment and best thinking follow. Reality is alive and well in an organization that engages employees like that, and reality never gets the chance to bite back.

Counseling Leaders About Communications

A public relations and communications forum I once attended kicked around the question of why CEOs don't always heed our advice. Good question. But the answer is not simple, and none of the participants' responses were brief. Their personal anecdotes spoke volumes. Let me share my answer here by way of my own first-hand experience a number of years ago.

The CEO of a multi-site manufacturing firm asked for our help regarding an evolving internal situation. This unionized environment was facing stiff offshore competition, a new and increasingly challenging threat that was stealing long-time customers. But the employees didn't appear to be responding with appropriate urgency. The CEO wanted us to assess the internal environment and make recommendations to achieve the desired behavior changes.

During our early visits, we spoke with the senior leaders one at a time to get a sense of the story behind the story, the messages they had been trying to get out to the employee audience, and through what means. We were taken aback by something the CEO said. With complete confidence and seriousness, he told us that his messages were well understood across the organization. When we asked how he knew that, he acted as though the question was absurd. He essentially told us that, because he was the CEO, and he had said what he had said, it was therefore heard and understood.

Overlooking his overt arrogance and naïveté, we sought and received permission to conduct informal discussions with groups of employees at several locations to determine whether the key messages were, in fact, getting through to the intended audience and, more important, whether those messages were understood.

As we soon learned, the CEO was wrong. What he thought he was communicating achieved nearly the opposite effect of what he had sought. There was a communications disconnect somewhere in the company, a barrier to the full import of leadership messages reaching their target audience with their intended effect. In the end, the urgent messages about the changing competitive environment were being met with skepticism and, in some quarters, open ridicule.

After a thorough analysis, we presented our findings to the CEO, along with recommendations for implementing an aggressive new employee engagement strategy intended to address the credibility problem head-on. He thanked us for our work, promised to study our recommendations, and said he would get back to us.

Fast-forward twelve months. Since we hadn't heard from the CEO or his team, we assumed they had digested and implemented our recommendations without our assistance, which was certainly their prerogative. So imagine our surprise when he called us in a panic. Union negotiators had walked out of contract talks for its biggest factory and had threatened to strike if their terms were not met. How could we help?

As we learned, our recommendations had not been implemented, and management's lack of credibility had continued to erode until it reached a flash point around contract talks into which they had tried to inject marketplace realities for a new, less restrictive contract.

The union negotiators opposed what it perceived as "give-backs" and were arguing their case to the public in the local news media. Meanwhile, the company remained silent publicly, refusing comment when the media sought it, operating under the belief that the contents of the private negotiations were not for public discussion – even though the union wasn't operating that way. The result was a one-sided story, with the company portrayed as the bad guy.

After completing a situation analysis, we helped the management team go public with the full story, countering the union's case point-by-point through a series of full-page "advertorials" in local newspapers, as well as face-to-face meetings between the CEO with his company negotiating team and the local press.

The tide quickly turned, and the company regained control of the public dialogue. Ultimately, the new contract was approved with the necessary changes. But the original internal credibility problem still existed.

When the dust settled, we updated and reintroduced our year-old recommendations to address the inherent problem of credibility. This time, lesson learned, they were enacted.

So the short answer to the forum question is that, as outside consultants, we certainly hope and expect leadership to enact our recommendations. But in the end, the CEO will do what he/she thinks best in the larger context in which the company operates.

As outsiders with necessarily limited insights into the organization and its challenges, we must acknowledge that the CEO has access to much more information, some of it confidential, from a greater diversity of sources, as well as more constituencies to satisfy than do we. Like any advisor, we can only give the CEO our best thinking on the basis of our background, experience and knowledge, as well as our understanding of the circumstances he/she faces. After that, it's their call.

Build a Communications Responsibilities Pyramid

The conventional understanding of employee communications can sometimes be summed up in four words: "I speak. You listen."

In other words, some people believe that employee communications are simply top-down, with messages and information emanating from leadership and senior managers for consumption by the broad mass of employees. This approach assumes that

a) Individual employees will receive the message in its entirety, when they are supposed to receive it.
b) They will understand it and what it means to them.
c) They will know what to do as a result of getting it.
d) They will act accordingly.

Unfortunately, it doesn't work that way. Assumptions like that are haughty. They have a tendency to sneak up behind one making the assumption and surprise them when they least expect it, and the result is never good for the business.

Effective employee engagement and communications entail responsibilities for everyone in the organization, from the CEO to the individual front line employee; a hierarchy that develops and sustains on-going dialogues, discussion, and debate up, down, and across the organization, among and between leadership, managers, supervisors, and employees.

A few years ago, we were working with a client and helped them see the truth in this, then helped them implement it (to their enormous benefit, I might add). The responsibilities pyramid we developed with them, with a few tweaks, could be adopted for any organization's communications.

It begins in the executive suite with an aspirational vision for the organization, the establishment of a strategy to realize that vision, management of strategy execution, the story behind the vision and strategy, and the rules of engagement – i.e., how the business and people will operate in the quest.

For their part, managers' responsibility is to comprehend and activate the strategy, interpreting it for their respective teams and/or business units or functional areas to make it relevant, then engage their teams regularly to make it real.

Managers must also establish mid-point and end targets for their teams to aim for, how they will measure progress toward those targets, and adjust as events and needs dictate. To this last point, that means that managers must pay attention to where the business is going, where their industry is headed, the effects of competition and the current economy on both, and how employees are impacted.

Developing and disseminating this content, by the way, on a regular basis is a critical responsibility of the company's communications professionals. At the same time, managers must encourage a two-way conversation by asking employees the right questions and jointly identifying problems, challenges, opportunities, and gaps early.

The last wedge of the responsibilities pyramid, employees, is the one most often overlooked. Yet, without it, communications, no matter how well planned, will fail.

Employees must be encouraged to be independent thinkers.

They need to be actively engaged in the business at all times, conscious of its health as well as that of its market and industry. Employees must be active listeners, with a strong desire for continuous learning. And last, rather than just bring problems to their supervisors, they must pose ideas, suggestions, and solutions. This set of responsibilities is key. This is employee engagement.

It's not enough just to announce a directive that employees must be engaged. Employee engagement in a healthy operation is a continuous state of affairs where information flows readily up, down, and across the organization, without a lot of impediments or formalities about who can and cannot talk to whom. It's where people feel valued, regardless of their role; where their ideas, suggestions, and solutions are welcomed, even if they can't be acted on for whatever reason.

This state is cultivated always, in good times and bad.

Employees are emotionally tied to the business, conscious of their own connection to its welfare and how their performance contributes to its success, or failure, and, by extension, to their personal success or failure.

In organizations like this, their good work is rewarded, not just with promotions and pay increases but also with recognition and acknowledgement. In the end, isn't that why we do what we do, to contribute to and be part of a healthy, thriving organization, and be appreciated for it?

Gain More Value From Your Meetings

Like the weather, everyone complains about meetings, but no one does anything about it. But can they?

Meetings are huge consumers of the average business day, whether in-person around a conference table or over the phone using webcasts or a web conferencing service. Many people consider them mostly a waste of time. Those feelings are often justifiable. And that's unfortunate, because meetings can be among the most valuable communications tools. They need not be time wasters.

In that communication is the on-going exchange of ideas, information and insights among people that leads to better understanding, meetings can and should be the most effective form of communication in a business environment. Unlike emails bouncing around or voice mails that may wait days for responses, meetings enable the right people to get together to share ideas and information, then make necessary decisions on the spot, in real time.

Unfortunately, it doesn't always work out that way. Some meetings are poorly planned and executed. Key people straggle in late or leave early. Participants digress or argue over minor unrelated details. People come unprepared. Meetings run late. Decisions are postponed repeatedly.

No wonder so many people think they're a waste of time.

Let's start with the fact that some meetings may not even be necessary. That being the case, it's imperative to establish some ground rules and a litmus test to justify holding meetings, and urge everyone to abide by them. Following are some rules and guidelines I've found helpful.

- One person takes charge, coordinating and securing a convenient meeting time and location; identifying the right attendees, ensuring they are invited and informed of the meeting's purpose and agenda; facilitating the discussion; and handling any necessary follow-up.

- One-hour meetings seem to be the norm, but if your agenda is long and complicated, extend it. Better to plan long and end the meeting early than to run late. Ending ahead of schedule is "found" time for participants. (Just don't make it a habit. Rather, plan the time slot better next time.)

- What is the meeting's purpose? Simply put, the meeting should serve as an efficient means to exchange information and ideas on a particular topic among three or more people on the way to reaching understanding and/or decisions. The purpose should be clearly spelled out in the invitation.

- Though most meetings' purpose is to reach decisions or agreements, that's not a requirement. Information exchanges can justify get-togethers where attendees bring ideas, insights and information from different corners of the organization for the benefit of all. Informational meetings also help bring newcomers and outsiders (e.g., consultants) up to speed quickly.

- Who should come? Are all invitees necessary? If you've been in large meetings, you know a meeting's effectiveness decreases and its duration increases with each additional participant. Do all attendees have something to contribute, either in terms of information and ideas or decision-making authority?

- What is the monetary cost of your meeting? Just to keep things in perspective, take a minute to make a ballpark estimate. Do some quick math to figure out the salary cost of holding the meeting, based on the approximate average salary of the attendees. Let's assume you've invited ten people to your one-hour meeting and their average annual salary is $100,000. The cost in terms of salary for your meeting then would be $500. And that doesn't include the unknown and hidden costs, such as lost opportunity costs (i.e., what they might have accomplished while not in the meeting). Consider these cost angles when deciding whom to invite to your meeting. No sense in inviting the whole department if it isn't necessary.

- If others require information from the meeting, but would have little or nothing to contribute, such as your boss, don't invite them (though you might want to let your boss disinvite him/herself). Inform them later of what came out of the meeting in terms of decisions or actions to be taken, and whether (and how) the decisions impact them.

- Establish an agenda, distribute it with the invitation, and stick to it. In addition to discussion topics, the agenda should include both starting and ending times. Hold firmly to that so that attendees can plan their own time accordingly.

- Stay on topic. If participants digress or spend too much time on one narrow subject, re-center the discussion and suggest a second meeting later for just those people. Discourage side discussions.

- Before the meeting starts, ask attendees to turn off their smartphones. I don't care what people say about their unique multi-tasking prowess. Anyone who's checking email on his or her iPhone during your meeting is not paying attention. (See *"Be Present in the Moment,"* page 149, for more on this point.)

- Ask participants to avoid repeating or rephrasing what has already been said unless they have something genuinely new or unique to add. When people feel they need to weigh in on every comment, the meeting bogs down, dragging on far longer than necessary. People get bored and start checking their watches.

- Never close a meeting without consensus on clearly delineated decisions and/or actions, with assigned responsibilities.

- Finish the meeting on time. If it looks like the meeting will run late, seek attendees' permission to extend it. But if that proves impractical for them, reschedule a follow-up.

- A follow-up meeting may be necessary if incomplete information prevented a decision. If so, identify the people responsible for gathering the necessary information and assign a deadline. Schedule a second meeting (if necessary).

- Follow up. Keep minutes, if appropriate, and distribute them to attendees, with emphasis on unfinished business and action items. Even if you don't keep formal minutes, at least provide a post-meeting summary to all attendees, especially including actions that need to be taken and who is responsible for what.

- Reconnect later with those who've been assigned action items. Make sure they are able to meet their deadlines. If they require additional resources or time, help them get the necessary help and inform the other participants of the need to postpone the follow-up meeting.

Those whose daily business lives are filled with meetings may find some of these rules and guidelines obvious. But your colleagues and managers will hold you in greater esteem if you consciously apply them to your own meetings, and, your organization will operate more effectively.

Reach People Where They Are

Much of my work involves helping clients better understand and appreciate how people within their organizations communicate, and how they prefer to get the information their companies want them to have. Gaining insights into those issues comprise the first steps toward developing a communications model that effectively reaches the internal audiences.

There is no single solution, not even within one individual company. The legwork must be done, preferably by getting out and talking directly to the employees at all levels.

One of my first lines of inquiry when talking with employees in that context is to determine their reading and listening habits, and how they get the information they want and need, both for personal and business purposes. (In fact, their personal habits often mirror their preferences within the business environment, which is why I ask.)

Where do they go to get their news? When there's a big breaking news story, to what source do they turn first? Which sources do they trust the most (and least)? How do they stay informed about the issues that concern them? How does that parallel the ways they get the information they need on the job, or does it? How would they prefer to get the kind of on-the-job information that helps them perform their jobs?

Establishing a pattern among a particular employee audience is critical in developing a communications strategy that reaches them in a timely fashion to assure that important management messages are getting through, and that those messages are relevant to them and their world.

But what are we to make of the growing reality that the general population is apparently becoming increasingly reading- and information-averse? Not only that, but the sharp audience declines experienced by most print and broadcast news media seem to indicate a growing distaste for conventional news sources. So where are people going now for their news? Or do they even care?

Of course, the answer largely depends on which demographic you're talking about. Gauging by the types of advertising that predominate the evening network newscasts (geriatric medications, mobility devices, and such) it's safe to conclude that the older demographic is tuning in.

Many among the younger generations, the fastest growing demographic and the one that increasingly comprises companies' internal audience, gets much of its news from faux news broadcasts like Comedy Central's "The Daily Show," as well as the late night talk show hosts' opening comedic monologues and guest interviews. That helps explain the scramble among politicians, even sitting presidents and presidential candidates, to be guests on those shows: that's where the target audience is.

I raise the subject because of a self-described "rant" by prolific blogger and marketer Seth Godin on this very topic. After reading it, I was led to do a little online research. I am an inveterate book reader and newspaper consumer, so I find it troubling to learn that the average person spends about seventy seconds each day reading the news *online*. A 2014 the U.S. Bureau of Labor Statistics study showed that the average American spends only 19 minutes a day reading, and that those between the ages 25 and 34 read for just eight minutes a day. Teenagers spend just four minutes a day reading on non-school days, according to the same study.

This is verified by my own observations, particularly when I see young businesspeople (though not exclusively young) in airport waiting lounges. What are they doing with this idle time? When they're not talking on their cell phones, checking email on their smartphones, working on a laptop, or playing video games on some kind of hand-held device, it's likely they're staring off into space or napping. No book, no newspaper, and no magazine, that's for sure.

Do you remember the TV advertisement a number of years ago for Nintendo's old hand-held Gameboy video game player? The businessman at the crowded airport gate got the bad news that his flight was, once again, delayed. He grinned, continued playing with his Gameboy and, without looking up, gave a one-word response to the gate agent: "*Cool!*"

These facts depress me, knowing that people are less well informed, apparently "deliberately ignorant" of current affairs, to quote Seth Godin. At the same time, these facts tell us that we need to adjust and broaden our approaches to internal communications vehicles if we are to reach our employees with any regularity, if we are to make sure all of them get the information we want them to have.

We must delve deeply to learn their reading habits (or lack thereof) and strive to be ever more creative in our selection and use of communications channels and tools, as well as how we craft our messages.

No longer can we assume that printed newsletters, mass distribution of emails, or even "town hall meetings" are the best (or only way) to reach the broad employee audience with our critical messages. I cringe at the recollection of a former client for whom the *only* means of reaching its worldwide employee audience was through emails. We discovered that a number of employees used their spam filters to sift out the frequent emails they received from corporate headquarters, which they deemed largely irrelevant and a waste of their time.

Instead, we must tailor our communications approaches to accommodate our audience's evolving habits, to meet our people on territory familiar and comfortable to them – territory that may not be familiar and comfortable for us, the communicators.

That may mean overcoming our discomfort with and lack of trust in the social media where many younger employees spend so much time: Facebook, Twitter, YouTube, and the like in their free time. At the same time, we need to be cognizant of other employees, often the older ones, for whom these social media are alien, who may perceive them as frivolous time-wasters.

There are business versions of these well-known social media, including Facebook's own "Workplace," a virtual twin platform for password-restricted use within an organization. Another popular internal platform is Yammer.

The point is, if we want to have an on-going dialogue with employees about what's important to the business, we need to engage them where they are, not where we wish they were.

Advertising Can Sell Your Employees, Too

When a marketer advertises during the Super Bowl, what kind of message is it sending to its internal audience, its employees?

This is a pertinent question that doesn't always get asked, which was even more relevant in 2008 when businesses were struggling with sinking revenues and declining profitability. Layoffs at the larger companies, the kind that advertise during the Super Bowl, had been common in those years. And those that were not cutting staff were asking their employees to pinch pennies.

So in a weak economic climate when a penny-pinching company spends millions of dollars on Super Bowl advertising (which in those years cost more than $3 million for a thirty-second spot), do employees resent it and see it as hypocritical, contrary to a climate of cost cutting? Perhaps. But there's another angle to this. And while the decision to forego high profile advertising in the name of cost-savings may seem obvious, it isn't.

According to an article in *The Wall Street Journal* in November 2008, this was a question that FedEx wrestled with in the midst of a hiring and spending freeze. The package-delivery giant had advertised in each of the previous twelve Super Bowls and had reserved a slot for the 2009 game, as did a number of other advertisers. In fact, NBC's inventory of ad spots was fully reserved by September 2008. But that was before the financial meltdown.

Though FedEx ultimately decided not to advertise in that Super Bowl, a spokesperson said prior to announcing the final decision that it was concerned that spending such an exorbitant amount of money when it was "asking employees to do more with less" would not be received well.

I remember, a number of years ago, a beautiful advertisement for Porsche in a number of glossy magazines. The ad featured a large double gatefold with a schematic cut-away of the Porsche 911 and intricate airbrush graphics detailing all the unique engineering that makes a Porsche so special.

At the time, when I was a neophyte in the marketing business, I doubted the expensive advertisement sold many cars. But a wiser marketer who reviewed the campaign in *Advertising Age* magazine explained it a different way. The ad wasn't meant so much to sell new cars as it was to confirm to Porsche owners that they had made the right decision.

It gave owners a private little gloat, and made them proud of their decision, and their exceptional machine. It provided them more information about their cars than they had ever gotten, facts and details that underlined the thrill they experienced using the product, while sealing their loyalty.

In the same way, advertising a product or service in bad economic times may, on the surface, seem frivolous and wasteful, especially to the insiders who are having to deal with the effects of belt-tightening.

And so a case can certainly be made for skipping the Super Bowl and putting those millions to better use inside the company and/or assuring continued customer support.

The opposite case can also be made. A high-profile Super Bowl ad, done correctly, can send a message of strength, determination, conviction, and renewed faith in the firm's future. It says to employees that "we're in it for the long haul, come what may.

We're not going away." That's certainly an important message to the employees as they fight to keep the firm profitable and worry about the vulnerability of their jobs in tough financial times. It can steel their resolve when they get a morale boost like that. Like the Porsche ad, it can seal the deal with the employees.

But make no mistake about it: it's a delicate decision, one that needs to be thought out in the larger context of marketing goals and the company's long-term strategic direction, just as does the tone of the advertisement. The very decision itself to advertise and the rationale behind that decision need to be communicated internally to the employees so that they understand the ad's value to the company.

While the chief marketing officer and his/her team (with the senior management likely weighing in) often make the decision, another voice ought to be heard in that process – the internal communications professionals.

Questions about the value of the highly visible advertisement in the context of the internal climate must be posed and considered in terms of, not only the ultimate decision of whether to advertise, but how to advertise, the content, and the tone. The wise marketer will accommodate and honor that input. The company will be stronger for it, regardless of the ultimate decision.

Break Down the Walls to Improve Communications

One truth I've learned in my years in employee communications, a truth often cited in this book, is the value of bringing the outside in. For a business to succeed and thrive, its people must remain ever aware of how evolving external influences impact their organization, both directly and indirectly, for better or for worse.

Of particular importance are the shifting paradigms that can mean new competition, changing consumer tastes and unexpected economic forces that result in new demands on employees and their companies. It might include competitors' actions (new products, etc.), the state of the economy (a persistent recession), and regulatory changes and new taxes that can complicate business and add costs.

While that's of central importance, equally critical is a company's ability to bring together functions within the company itself, to cross-fertilize internally as well.

People in one function need to have an on-going awareness of what the other functions are doing, particularly as they may impact their own area. At the same time, their unit's operation ought to be better understood across the business.

For instance, do people in marketing fully understand the challenges faced by R&D or manufacturing? And vice-versa? Do the people in R&D have a keen sense of customers' desires and the kinds of features they may be expecting in the next product iteration? Is the product development operation conscious of the fiscal constraints that an ailing economy is placing on the company?

Does finance have an appreciation of why product promotion might cost as much as it does or why procurement costs are rising? Does finance understand why the human resources department needs an increase in its recruitment and training budgets during an economic recession?

No doubt the senior managers in charge of those functional areas know and appreciate the answers, but what about the people within their units? Is everyone operating in a vacuum?

I'm reminded of an old Dilbert cartoon where, in a meeting, the marketing manager presents a fancy brochure for a new product. When Dilbert points out that the company doesn't even make the product, the marketing guy responds, "That hasn't hurt our sales so far."

Communications professionals play a central role in helping create and open up the avenues between functions to assure that people understand what's going on in other parts of the organization; that they fully grasp the evolving internal dynamic and how what they do and the decisions they make may impact what goes on in other parts of the company.

In some quarters, this is referred to as "breaking down the silos" that exist in every organization. But it's about more than just eliminating silos. It's about reaching across those natural divides, and not just at senior management retreats where the functional and operational vice presidents share ideas, insights, challenges, and opportunities.

It must be a robust, on-going dialogue at all levels. And it needn't be time-consuming. Maybe it's no more than managers establishing the links and encouraging dialogue. Maybe it's an occasional spontaneous lunch in the cafeteria between a half-dozen people from different departments, just to shoot the breeze. It's amazing what those informal, friendly conversations can open up, the kinds of ideas they stimulate and, perhaps most important, the relationships they spawn.

When functions operate independently, it can only spell trouble. In September 2004, Oprah Winfrey gave away 276 new GM Pontiac G6 sedans to members of her studio audience. GM scored quite a PR coup. But it was a short-lived triumph. When intrigued Oprah viewers went to their local Pontiac dealers hoping to test drive or buy a G6, they were disappointed. None were in the showroom, and none would be available for several months. What might have been a huge sales surge for Pontiac fell flat on its face.

If Pontiac's promotional gurus had better coordinated their planning with manufacturing, they might have learned that production of the G6 was not going to ramp up fully for another half-year. So Oprah might have postponed her give-away until the following year, and Pontiac likely would have sold several thousand more cars. Need I point out what has happened to Pontiac in the intervening years? Probably a coincidence, but still…

This doesn't have to be overly complicated. It simply requires an attitude of curiosity across the organization, where people want to know what is going on around the company, not just what the guy at the adjacent desk is doing.

There can and should be numerous ways to oxygenate the organization. No single way is right or wrong. An internal newsletter helps, as does an information-rich and frequently updated intranet news service.

But nothing can substitute for actively getting to know the other folks and what's on their minds. It's amazing what can be learned just by talking and listening.

Keep Employees Engaged
Through The Tough Times

In a war zone or the scene of a natural disaster, triage is a means of prioritizing critically injured people for appropriate treatment based on their relative need for care. It's a supply-and-demand challenge— too many patients and too few doctors, nurses and operating rooms. Triage efficiently rations patient care in the context of insufficient resources to assure the best possible outcomes, though that does not necessarily mean optimal medical treatment for all.

Various inter-related considerations go into deciding who gets treatment and who gets it first. The number of patients versus the number of available medical personnel and equipment is the first consideration.

Those gravely injured but with a chance of survival if treated immediately are given priority. Those least likely to survive are usually given enough attention to assure a modicum of comfort, but little more. Less severe cases are put on hold until the more endangered cases are stabilized.

In difficult economic situations, many businesses practice their own version of triage as they continue to bleed cash and customers.

For instance, many retail chains will shutter under-performing stores that became an over-extension of their ability to serve ever fewer customers. These outlets are unlikely to see a near-term reversal of fortune, while they continue to deplete precious cash flow. They must be pared from the system.

Internally, countless other triage-like decisions are made that impact all facets of the operation. Early on, when the revenue drop first becomes apparent, decisions focus on the so-called "low-hanging fruit," cutting back on or not doing things deemed superfluous or luxuries, such as regional sales conferences, certain training activities, and some travel and entertainment.

Of course, when those kinds of cutbacks are found to be insufficient to stop the bleeding, additional steps are taken, such as reducing or eliminating overtime and salary freezes, followed by asking people to take pay cuts. The very last resort is to lay off full-time employees, akin to a medical amputation.

"Amputation" is not hyperbolic. After having invested in hiring, training, and cultivating employees and their commitment, cutting them loose represents a repudiation of those not insignificant outlays. And, when business picks up again, as it usually does, those investments will need to be made all over again.

While it's certainly understandable to offset corporate losses by cutting back on expenses, it's unwise to make generalizations about where, what, and how to cut, especially when it comes to outside consultants, including those who provide communications counsel.

Certainly in the context of triage-style layoffs, the retention of outsiders doesn't play well among the remaining employees. People may ask, "Why is the company still spending money on consultants after it laid off long-time employees?"

It's a valid question, but communications consultants can help managers prepare for and deal with the chaos and uncertainty spawned by cutbacks and layoffs. Further, unlike full-time employees, the cost of consultants is a short-term investment and does not require additional outlay and overhead costs, such as benefits and office space.

Communications counsel can help managers in their quest to engage employees, and build and sustain strong employee relationships and trust through good times and bad, but especially during bad times. As noted in *Re-engage Employees After the Layoffs* (page 27), wage and hiring freezes and layoffs result in nervous and insecure employees everywhere, not always able to do their best work, which is the last thing a stressed organization needs. Businesses need their people to be at their best to tackle today's complex challenges and can't afford disaffected or disconnected employees.

Managers and leaders must take some simple actions to counteract the unavoidably negative climate of fear that can set in and afflict even the best businesses under the cloud of budget cuts or a recent (or potential) layoff.

Managers and leaders must reach out to the workforce frequently, especially face-to-face; re-engage them in the business at hand by reaffirming business goals and the strategies that will get you there; remind them why the company is in business; and bring in the outside world to re-emphasize the climate of uncertainty under which the company is operating, including the challenges being faced by customers, suppliers and competitors.

Leadership should keep managers in the loop so there is a common understanding of the marketplace realities, the company's business strategy going forward, and the responsibilities of the employees to drive results. Managers should be encouraged to stay informed about the external forces and current events that impact their company directly and indirectly. And they should talk to their teams regularly about these realities and their effects.

Communications departments should fill the pipeline with relevant news and information, along with guidance as to how best to use it.

Difficult times demand superior performance from everyone to help minimize the damage that a poor economy might visit upon an organization. Companies cannot afford to have employees distracted by fear of job loss. Successful companies are those that keep employees engaged in the challenges at hand by communicating with them often and keeping them apprised of evolving situations.

Conversely, when employees are kept in the dark, left to read the tealeaves and draw their own conclusions, they usually infer the worst and operate accordingly.

Good communications go a long way toward keeping key people engaged in the tasks at hand, facing challenges head-on with their best skills and talents. Companies that truly engage their people in the business challenges are those that will emerge from a weak economy the strongest.

Tell a Clear, Coherent Story

Organizations going through significant change risk the imminent danger of people losing focus on the central mission, lacking a full appreciation for and understanding of the change, its impact on the company and on them, and, most important, their role in the transformational process.

That kind of result is understandable since organizational change often involves doing things in new ways and discarding outmoded practices. People can easily become disoriented.

A clearly delineated story about your company, its purpose, and where it's going in dealing with change will help you focus your organization's best talents on what matters most, thereby helping to drive meaningful results.

Profound organizational change typically accompanies a merger or acquisition, external shifts in the markets in which the company operates, or response to a new competitive threat. Similarly, change occurs when there is new top leadership, when a new CEO brings with him/her a new management team and a new strategic direction.

Whenever internal or external forces impose abrupt transformation on an organization, it's critical that employees quickly gain a clear understanding of the change and get their bearings so that their talents, energies, and thinking are focused on the right things as soon as possible. The alternative is a lot of wasted energy focused on mundane matters of little or no consequence to the company's new mandate and sense of urgency. Worse, companies' most talented and valuable people can become disillusioned and disconnected, focusing their energies instead on finding new employment elsewhere.

The best and quickest route to keep people on board, moving proactively toward the new challenges, is through the development and deployment of a narrative that tells the new story clearly and succinctly, then making sure it's used consistently across the organization.

The narrative is a distillation of the appropriate words, phrases, and descriptors of the change, including:

- what it is and the rationale behind it;
- the external and/or internal forces that mandate the change;
- how the organization must adapt;
- where the change will likely take the company; and
- the internal and external facts that support the change in direction and the company's chosen strategic response.

Narratives enable managers at all levels to gain quick employee understanding of what exactly has to change in the company and their jobs, and why. The narrative helps managers interpret and make relevant the change for their own particular unit in terms of what people need to do differently, appropriate to where the company as a whole needs to go. To borrow a tired old cliché, it gets everyone rowing in the same direction.

Consensus of the company's leadership and communications professionals creates the narrative. It provides them and all managers with consistent language to help them talk about the change and its impact on and importance to the entire organization, as well as the individual operational and functional units, and employees.

Individual employees, then, more readily connect their role and responsibility to the larger picture, able to see the link between what they do and where the organization now needs to go, then how they need to change what they do to support that.

An apt metaphor for an organization going through such change is an aircraft carrier. There are hundreds of unique jobs on a typical carrier, all toward the common mission of delivering a navy's forward strike capabilities.

The carrier's mission changes often. There may be a new attack target, the carrier might be directed to a new port, or weather changes may force it to be repositioned. If an attack is called for, the carrier must get itself as near the action as possible, as quickly as possible, then position itself into the wind to assure that the fighter and attack jets achieve maximum lift for their short takeoffs. To do that demands precise execution by countless officers and sailors assigned to a range of jobs.

So when the carrier's mission changes, everyone must take the new mission into account in what he or she must do, how, and when it must be done. The commander's job is to delegate to his officers the task of making the mission's story relevant to their respective crews so that each crew performs its tasks appropriately, precisely, and in a coordinated manner.

As often as an aircraft carrier's mission may change, it's not an overstatement to compare its rate of change to that of a business organization. In this age, amid the current economic turmoil and uncertainties, companies must remain nimble, able to tack and change course constantly, just like an aircraft carrier.

So what's your story? As your company's mission changes to accommodate market fluctuations, a new acquisition, or a new strategic direction, that change will similarly impact what people do, how they do it, and when. Your ability to tell a clear, coherent story will prove to be an invaluable tool, assuring that managers across operations and functions are well informed and plugged into the organization's new direction. And well-informed managers, with a clear narrative at hand, can make that new mission relevant and meaningful to their teams, helping them stay on course.

Listen to the Customer's Voice

The role of a company's employee communications operation is, by its name and nature, almost exclusively focused inside the organization. Yet, expanding its responsibilities to the company's other critical audience – its customers – can reap benefits beyond measure.

That's not to say that communications managers should take on marketing communications responsibilities, too. Rather, they should serve as a dialogue facilitator and conduit to the customers' world to help the internal audience gain a better appreciation for and greater insights into the world of the customer.

Consider your own experiences receiving shoddy treatment at a retail store, versus the outstanding service you may have gotten elsewhere. Why the difference? It's not purely happenstance that one experience is consistently great while the other is often lousy.

The difference between the two is likely the success (or lack thereof) that the respective organizations have had in getting their employees to appreciate the needs and desires of their customers, the challenges they face, and the reason those customers come to them in the first place for fulfillment of their needs or solutions to their challenges.

A business exists to provide greater ease and comfort for its customers by making their lives simpler on some level, satisfying some desire or need they may have, or addressing challenges they can't resolve on their own. If the people in your organization who deal directly with your customers aren't doing that effectively, consistently and courteously, if they are in fact doing the opposite, then organizational failure can't be far behind.

Think back to bad experiences you've had with businesses, big and small. Are those organizations still in business? Have they declared bankruptcy, been acquired or just folded? Without naming names, I can think of a few that got their just deserts.

In helping my clients improve their employees' appreciation for the world of the customer, I've done the legwork on their behalf in a few cases. The pay-off in each instance was huge – far more impactful than the client had expected.

In two different cases, both industrial companies selling products and services to other businesses, I worked with the sales managers to bring the real world of their customers to the sales team.

I grabbed my videocam and conducted interviews with a dozen or so different customers at their sites, asking them about their needs, frustrations, and challenges, as well as how our clients and their competitors were or were not measuring up. The raw footage was edited down to cohesive 15-minute videos for their annual sales team meetings.

The impact was immediate and stunning. Both videos stimulated robust and productive discussions. Salespeople who called on these customers were hearing things they'd never heard before – or perhaps they hadn't listened closely enough.

The value of such insights doesn't pertain only to salespeople and those with direct customer contact. It can be meaningful to everyone in the organization, including back office support personnel, human resources managers, product developers, and manufacturing employees. How better for people to get a sense of why they do what they do, and how they might do it better?

There was another case where I helped make a similar customer video that was shown across the organization, even to people without direct customer contact. Especially telling was how the IT department gleaned important insights into the customers' experiences with the company. As a result, they enacted some comprehensive changes to the company's software that would improve the ability of customers to check their account status online, and give them access to information that had not previously been readily available. The IT folks had never realized those kinds of data were important to customers.

Businesses are launched with a vision of meeting previously unsatisfied needs. If that business succeeds at doing that to the point where it grows, but then loses touch with its original purpose and gets too big to continue doing that effectively, then what's the point of being in business?

The most difficult challenge any company faces in a growth mode, or even just staying ahead of the competition, can be maintaining that awareness and insight into the customer experience among its entire employee population, month after month, year after year.

To the extent that the company's employee communications professionals can help sustain and enhance that could be its most valuable contribution to the perpetuation and success of that organization.

Leadership Lessons

"If you're ridin' ahead of the herd,

take a look back every now and then

to make sure it's still there."

Will Rogers
Humorist, Actor, Commentator
1879 – 1935

How One CEO Communicated Effectively

In January 2001, as President-elect George W. Bush began forming his cabinet, he selected Paul H. O'Neill, then CEO of Alcoa, to become Treasury Secretary. As is its habit, *The New York Times* featured an extensive profile in its January 16, 2001, edition that, as it turned out, intrigued me not so much for its political theater, but rather for unintended the lesson it gave me in leadership communications.

It was a compelling story that I've kept all these years. On occasion, I share it with clients and colleagues as an example of effective executive communications that broke the mold of what people usually think of as "communications."

As the article noted, O'Neill was known for his business acumen. He came to Alcoa in the late 1980s from International Paper where he had been president. Alcoa then was on the ropes, losing money, closing plants and laying off workers. What struck me was the way O'Neill turned around Alcoa and the role that his unique approach to communications played in that reversal, communications that consisted of conscious actions and a sincere concern for employees.

In 1987, at the time of O'Neill's assumption of the role of CEO, the global aluminum business was struggling in the midst of a commodity glut and price war. O'Neill directed Alcoa to reduce production rather than the route his predecessor had taken, which was to cut prices. But he had a longer-term vision that he began to execute in the context of the downturn. O'Neill articulated shared corporate values and the importance of building internal consensus. And he leveraged the simple issue of worker safety to do it.

As the *Times* article noted, "O'Neill engineered a financial turnaround . . . [by] promoting worker safety as a way of improving productivity. . ." An Alcoa director observed that the approach served to inspire employees, "build coherence, and enlist the passions of his staff."

When he took over, his predecessor had been putting the final touches on a plan that would diversify the company. O'Neill deep-sixed the plan and, instead, broke up the company's command and control structure, substituting twenty autonomous units, each reporting directly to him, to respond better to customers.

He also cut back on the excesses that had taken root in the company's culture, selling corporate limousines and jets, cancelling executives' company-sponsored country club memberships, and the like. He also moved his office out of the executive suite and into cubicles among staff. But his major focus was on improving productivity, and that's where his focus on worker safety came into play.

Certainly worker safety is a critical issue in any industry, particularly one like aluminum production. But O'Neill saw the benefits of safety beyond its obvious altruism – its potential impact on the company's bottom line. As he explained it, "*A production process that resulted in worker injuries was a flawed process, incapable of making high quality products efficiently and cost-effectively.*"

So he instilled safety into the company culture and made it the recurring theme of all his communications. More to the point, because he was the CEO and because he made worker safety important, it also became important to all his managers, and therefore important across the entire organization, which, incidentally, is a central feature of truly effective employee communications.

Regardless of the audience, including meetings with non-Alcoa people, he opened his speeches with a discussion of safety, not only about how he was improving it at Alcoa's plants, but also personalizing it to the audience members. Before launching into his speech, he would point out the emergency exits from the meeting rooms and explain why it was important to be aware of that.

He would also talk at length about the importance of safety in the workplace, even if the audience were Wall Street analysts whose primary interest lay in revenue and profit forecasts. His larger goal was creating a cultural change. "If I can unify employees on the obvious issue of safety," he told one audience, "then I can unify them behind return on investment and assets."

He certainly got the attention of the unions. He was focusing on an issue, workplace safety, that's always important to any union's leadership. Once he had their attention, he promised job security if the employees worked smarter and more efficiently. That led to revisions in rigid union contract language to enable greater on-the-job empowerment for the workers and, ultimately, increased productivity.

The effort paid off. When he started in 1987, Alcoa's work force numbered 59,000 while the company's annual revenues were $1.5 billion. By 2000, it employed 140,000 and posted revenues of $23 billion. The then-head of the United Steelworkers of America, George Becker, said that O'Neill's emphasis on worker safety was "very sincere" and "one of his strong points." Becker's observations underline the effectiveness of O'Neill's communications. It was his sincerity and the single-minded focus that got people's attention. Through those means, he was able to achieve the cultural shift necessary to remake Alcoa into a world power aluminum producer.

As this tale illustrates, there is no limit to how executives communicate, only one's imagination. The key is not so much the means or the subject matter as it is its relevance to the audience, in this case, personalizing the value of a safe workplace to the people most affected by it.

Fill in the blank. Pick a different audience. What issue will get their attention, especially if your communications on the subject are sincere and passionate like O'Neill's were about worker safety? I guarantee that you will connect with your audience and fully engage them in the business' vision. And you will likely see positive results on the bottom line.

Lessons from a Presidential Campaign

The ritual of the modern campaign for the U.S. presidency provides the kind of trials and pressures not unlike those faced by most corporate CEOs.

That includes managing massive budgets; creating and sustaining loyalty; dealing with sudden and often unexpected challenges and setbacks; selling a range of ideas to skeptical audiences; finding, selecting, and motivating quality senior managers; then developing trusting relationships with those top people so that important tasks and decisions can be delegated without any second thoughts or doubts.

In that context, then, it was revealing to read in the *Atlantic Monthly* that Hillary Clinton apparently fell short in most of those areas in her failed bid for the Democratic nomination in 2008.

The only conclusion the reader could draw after reading the 6,100-word article ("The Front Runner's Fall," by Joshua Green, *Atlantic Monthly*, September 2008) was that Ms. Clinton apparently lacked basic management skills as she made her run for the presidency. Reaching that conclusion leads to the follow-on: despite how you may feel about her and her politics, she probably was not presidential timber; perhaps in the future, but not in 2008.

At the same time, the parallel conclusion one might draw is that, in this day and age, candidates like John McCain and Barack Obama, in getting as far as they had, demonstrated those key management skills and both should be commended for that.

We may complain about the duration of these campaigns, now running more than two years, but one thing is certain: they truly test the mettle of the candidates, putting them through some pretty rough paces.

Certainly, glad-handing voters, eating fatty fried chicken and kissing babies in Mason City, IA, and Ossipee, NH, in the dead of winter is not the same as staring down Vladimir Putin across a conference room table. And deciding whether to run an attack ad is not the same as the decision to go to war. But this is a tough job en route to acquiring the world's toughest. On many levels, the campaign is good preparation in that it demands the ability to:

- Attract, build, and retain the necessary core talent pool to run a complicated process under severe budget and time constraints.
- Develop and firmly establish a core driving vision, and then stick with it.
- Develop and maintain the loyalty of hundreds of staffers and tens of thousands of volunteers.
- Create, staff and inspire at least fifty independent state organizations.
- Communicate core messages clearly and effectively.
- And to do it all under the constant scrutiny of the modern news media – including the Internet, especially.

Those who do it well enough to get the nomination of their party certainly deserve our respect, regardless of how we may feel about their politics or their ability to govern. But why did Hillary Clinton fall short? Pundits on both sides of the political spectrum long felt she had an honest shot at winning the Democratic nomination, and maybe even the presidency. Could her downfall have been her poor management skills, as cited in the *Atlantic Monthly* article? Joshua Green sums up the dysfunction early in his story:

> *"Clinton ran on the basis of managerial competence, on her capacity, as she liked to put it, to 'do the job from Day One.' In fact, she never behaved like a chief executive, and her own staff proved to be her Achilles' heel. What is clear from the internal documents is that Clinton's loss derived not from any specific decision she made, but rather from the preponderance of the many she did not make. Her hesitancy and habit of avoiding hard choices exacted a price that eventually sank her chances at the presidency."*

Green cites numerous cases where she hesitated, wouldn't make a decision, or left it to others, including her husband, the former president. Former GE CEO Jack Welch was always fond of saying that it isn't the wrong decisions that hurt you. It's the decisions you don't make.

Ms. Clinton also struggled with putting together an effective core team, one whose skills blended and complemented hers and one another. There was a lot of backstabbing, backbiting, and second-guessing going on, according to Green. Consequently, making a bad situation worse, there were no clear lines of authority, and Ms. Clinton couldn't or wouldn't fill the gaps, often failing to intervene in the frequent internal spats.

Therein lies an important lesson for businesspeople, especially managers who must make decisions, hire and fire people, cultivate talent, sustain loyalty, all in the on-going challenge of running a successful business. People become managers and progress up through the organization because they learn how to execute these important tasks and do them well. Then they get better as they progress in the organization.

Most businesses are structured in such a way that those who don't progress in their management skills don't climb the corporate ladder. We could say the same is true of presidential aspirants and modern presidential campaigns.

Use Failure as a Teachable Moment

The use of sports metaphors in business is a common and established practice. It's natural in the parallel context of competitive teams vying against one another for victory and supremacy.

Though the metaphor can be and often is taken too far, there are in fact a number of appropriate analogies where businesspeople can get operational ideas and lessons from the world of sports.

Managers can learn many lessons from coaches—how to bounce back from defeat; how to stay on top; how to maximize limited resources; and how best to communicate with their teams, to name just four.

In that light, what can we learn from coaches as to the appropriate leadership communications in the face of failure? Suppose your operation loses a major client due to fumbled service. Or your fourth quarter results meant your unit didn't make its annual sales budget.

Maybe your superstar sales team didn't hit its numbers, or a competitor's new product rollout caught you off-guard and they took a big bite out of your market share lead. Sure, the competition was tough. It usually is. Perhaps you face a weak market or a struggling economy.

If you're the one in charge, what's the right message to your people, through what means, and when? Football may provide some valuable insights for this challenge.

The National Football League, composed of thirty-two teams,

holds its playoffs in January, on the way to the Super Bowl championship in early February. The playoffs start with sixteen teams and end with one champion.

What about the other fifteen teams? How does a losing coach deal with that, and what does he say to his team after a disappointing defeat abruptly ends a once promising season, with the championship nearly in sight?

On the heels of an embarrassing rout in the first round of the NFL playoffs the first weekend of the January 2010 playoffs, I wondered about the locker room atmosphere of my favorite team, the New England Patriots. More to the point, what did Coach Bill Belichick tell his team after an unexpectedly lop-sided loss to the underdog Baltimore Ravens?

New England is the same team that went to four Super Bowls from the 2000 season through the 2009 season, winning three of them. Even in those years when they didn't go all the way, they always were highly competitive.

What a losing coach may say to the media after the loss can reveal some of his attitude and approach in the locker room. After his team's second-round 34-3 loss to the Minnesota Vikings, the Dallas Cowboys' then-coach Wade Phillips said that it "felt like an elevator falling all the way from the top."

That simile is accurate and instructive. As a team, the Cowboys had an on-and-off season in 2009. But at the end, they rode the elevator nearly to the top, winning most of their late-season games, only to get routed in the divisional playoff game.

It's a cliché to hear "you have nothing to be ashamed of," and other such attempts at encouragement and solace.

So what's the most constructive thing a coach or business leader can say to the team? What words and messages will salve wounded egos and encourage recommitment to the longer term? The losing locker room is neither the time nor place for blame placing or recriminations.

Instead, effective coaches with their eye on the long-term will recall the good work that had been done that season and the effort that got the team as far as it did. They will cite the outstanding individual performances, but not dwell on the errors and miscues of the loss. They will save that for later, for the one-on-one private conversations that must take place between the coach and those players in need of encouragement and corrective guidance.

The loser's locker room immediately after the loss is, in fact, the time and place for finding the good on which a foundation can be built to begin to motivate the team for future greatness. The immediacy of the moment right after the loss, while the sting of defeat is still fresh like tears on cheeks, is the right time and place to deliver such messages.

The coach able to comfort and encourage his dispirited players is the coach whose team is more likely to return to the playoffs again the next year with reinvigorated team members that quickly regain their self-confidence and sense of excellence.

My guess is that Bill Belichick excels at this challenge. Reticent and cranky in his post-game press conferences, this is a leader who, behind the scenes, quietly encourages, motivates and instructs his players year after year. It shows, too, in the Patriots' post-season record. In his first ten seasons as the Patriots' head coach, the team won more than seventy percent of its games and won three Super Bowl titles while missing the post-season playoffs only twice.

That's a record any business manager would envy.

The CEO as Communicator-in-Chief

When I was young and new to the business world, I thought that the higher one rises in a corporate hierarchy, the easier it gets. Boy, was I wrong! I was probably thinking myopically about executive perquisites, the plush carpeted C-Suite, the private jet, the corner office and all that goes with it. In fact, the opposite is true, as any senior-level manager will tell you.

In many ways, rising through a corporate structure doesn't relieve you of unpleasant or difficult tasks; it just adds more. It means you learn how things work and what makes an organization excel. Sometimes, you have to get your hands dirty, even if you sit on top of the pyramid.

In fact, leaders who disdain the dirty work likely will fail because they become out of touch with the organization they purport to run. I've seen instances of that, and they were not pretty.

A large component of the counsel I provide clients is based on those experiences – both good and bad leaders I've been exposed to. Business books that are full of real world anecdotes also provide valuable insights.

So when it comes to business books, I'm partial to those on leadership where the core message concerns the merits of good communications and hands-on leadership. That's one reason I like John Kotter's books on leadership so much. He recognizes the central importance played by consistent, relevant and continuous communications, and how hands-on leadership is the most effective kind of communications. In that regard, among the best I've read are "Shackleton's Way" by Margot Morrell and Stephanie Capparell, "Inside Steve's Brain" by Leander Kahney, and, as noted, anything written by John Kotter. To this category, I would add another: "Walk The Walk" by Alan Deutschman.

The counsel contained in this book leans heavily toward hands-on involvement by leaders, and the truth of the expression *"actions speak louder than words."* This book is full of relevant and telling anecdotes about real world business leaders who excel at direct involvement and communication.

One of my favorites from the book concerns the late Ray Kroc, founder of McDonald's. Deutschman relates how Kroc visited franchises frequently and, as he approached the restaurant, would pick up trash in the parking lot before even setting foot inside.

Cleanliness was Kroc's central tenet. He believed that clean restaurants would appeal to his customers, bring them back for repeat visits, and build loyalty. Of course, he was right.

He demonstrated his abiding belief in this truth by attending to it himself. As the CEO, he could have walked into the restaurant and told the manager that there was trash in the parking lot. Instead, by demonstrating his willingness to do it himself, he elevated the importance of the task. (Imagine being a McDonald's manager in Podunk and looking out the window one afternoon, only to see your CEO picking up trash in your parking lot! Uh oh.)

Implicitly and explicitly, he was saying that if something is important enough for the CEO to do himself, then it must be pretty darned important.

The chapter I found most insightful was the fourth, titled "You Share The Struggle And The Risk." Deutschman writes, "Sharing the struggle is vital for anyone who aspires to leadership, whether it's the CEO of a company with hundreds of thousands of employees or a front-line manager with less than a dozen people."

He cites Southwest Airlines, where supervisors are considered to be "player-coaches," ready at all times to help get the job done, from handling baggage to serving as gate agents at departure lounges.

Even the founding and former CEO, Herb Kelleher, was known to pitch in when it got busy. He notes that the arrangement has "strengthened the feelings of loyalty coming from teammates, who appreciate the extra help when they're in a crunch, and it's made the supervisors become better coaches because they understand the work's pressures and challenges first-hand." Deutschman adds, "Leaders can't fully grasp the situation until they've shared the struggle."

He quotes a Whole Foods manager who spoke a core truth of successful management: "People don't work for companies; they work for people." That simple observation reveals much about successful leadership.

The manager or leader who falls back on the vague concept of "the company" to drive loyalty and hard work rather than his/her personal and direct involvement has lost sight of the fact that the organization is, in fact, people working together toward a common goal.

To that point, he concludes the chapter by writing about the "royal visit," where the "CEO and top executives drop in to see their workers or perhaps toiling in a front-line job on a single day a year, for a few hours at most."

Of such behavior, Deutschman writes, "The real difference comes when a leader is obsessive about getting the first-hand view," unfiltered by those with an axe to grind, rather than putting on a show of being involved. The impetus for such involvement must be first and foremost to learn from the personal experience, not to pretend to care.

A large, 170,000-employee organization I worked with a few years ago, was fortunate to have one of those obsessive types of CEOs. With customer service phone centers scattered around the country, it was common lore to hear tales of how this CEO would drop in unannounced, usually entering unaccompanied through the back door to avoid fanfare. He would spend several hours mingling with employees, talking with them about their work and its challenges.

Believe me, employees can spot a phony a mile away. They know the difference between a leader who truly wants to learn something like this CEO, and one who just wants to work down his checklist of plant visits. If a leader's real reason for the front-line visit is the latter, he/she would be better off just staying in the corner office.

Communications Equal Improved Performance

Business people are busy today. Very busy. That has always been true, but more so now in the context of a persistently weak economy. Companies are struggling to maintain profitability, the components of which reside in every part of the organization: from maintaining good client/customer relations, to wringing maximum productivity and efficiency from production, to cutting expenses to the bone.

For the senior people, these pressures are compounded. They carry the weight of the company on their shoulders. You're doing them a favor when you can relieve them of some of their burdens. So the suggestion that leaders, managers and supervisors become better communicators, spending more time communicating with employees, is often met with incredulity and outright rejection.

Yet focusing a bit more on communicating with one's employees can help bring some of the relief and support that is so critical in such trying times. A true story helps illustrate this.

A few years ago, a paper company engaged us in an employee communications assignment. This company owned several paper mills around the world.

The northern Wisconsin mill where my story takes place was quite large and consisted of three paper machines, each running three shifts around the clock.

Like other such mills, a paper machine manager and his team of assistant managers and supervisors run each component operation, covering the various facets of keeping that machine going. The manager of one machine in this mill told me this story and I've never forgotten it. One day, he went in for his annual physical. His doctor told him that he needed to get more exercise and suggested that a long walk each day would be a good start.

Like most paper mills, this mill is built with the offices at one end and an executive parking lot right outside. So this machine manager every day would walk perhaps one hundred feet between his car and his office. To follow his doctor's orders, however, he decided to park his car at the opposite end of the mill, forcing himself to walk the length of his paper machine, about a half-mile both morning and evening. Aside from getting more exercise, he realized some unexpected, but important benefits.

He suddenly had a lot more daily interaction with the people working on his paper machine than ever before. Sometimes it was a simple wave or nod and a "good morning" or "good night." Other times, it was talking about the latest NFL football game ("*How 'bout those Packers!*") or plans for the coming deer hunting or fishing season.

The important thing is that he broke the ice, whether he meant to or not. Over time, he also changed people's perceptions of who he was and what he did. He became more human and more approachable in their eyes. People increasingly felt comfortable coming to him on the floor with problems, ideas, insights and solutions. Though it hadn't been his original intention when he started his daily constitutionals, he opened lines of communication that had never before existed, in turn building mutual trust with the work force.

His was one of the older paper machines in the company. Yet, about a year after he began his daily walks through the plant, his operation's performance numbers rose markedly, so high in fact that it became the most productive and efficient operation in the entire company. What happened? Did communications play a role in making this production line suddenly so productive? I think you know the answer.

As this manager told me, as his people came to feel more comfortable with him, they told him things about his equipment and operation that he hadn't fully appreciated before. And when he engaged in a little give-and-take with these hands-on operators, they had ideas and insights that he, as the guy in charge, could and did act on.

Sitting in a remote office, buried in reports and emails, running from one meeting to the next, managers don't get a lot of opportunity to get their hands dirty, so to speak, learning what makes their operations tick. Or perhaps they allow that busy-ness to get in the way.

So the lesson here is, create the opportunity. Get out and talk to people. Pretend your doctor told you to do it. You may be surprised by what you learn.

Treat Your Employees as You Would Your Peers

Years ago, while impaneled as a jury member on a medical malpractice case against a practicing obstetrician, I learned an important lesson about people, a lesson applicable to employee relations and leadership communications.

This complicated medical malpractice case involved a lot of unfamiliar medical jargon from expert witnesses, as well as the physician defendant. I toiled to comprehend and link the various aspects of the case, to sift out the deeper significance of the testimony and separate the truths from the embellishments.

It didn't help that both the plaintiff and the defendant spoke with thick foreign accents or that the courtroom was lined with echo-inducing marble. But I was troubled by something else, too.

Frankly, because I was struggling to make sense of it, I was concerned about the ability of my fellow jurors to comprehend the complex details of the case and pass judgment appropriately. After the lawyers rested their cases, as we retired to the jury's chamber, it was clear to me that the doctor was innocent. I fully intended to vote that way. But I wondered about the other members of the jury.

In my cynical, college-educated view, I cast a skeptical eye at my fellow jurors. Ironically, while sitting with a panel of my peers in judgment of a doctor, I was instead passing judgment on those peers.

All but two jurors (myself and a young woman) were blue-collar workers. I assumed they had not been able to follow the details of the case and would likely cast a vote based on the emotions of the case, i.e., that they would find in favor of the plaintiffs because they would identify more with the poor working class woman and her husband (who was newly unemployed) than the (presumably) wealthy doctor, awarding them (and their lawyer) several million insurance company dollars.

Boy, was I ever wrong. It was a quick decision. On our first vote, we, the jury, unanimously found the doctor defendant not guilty.

One jury member suggested it would be inappropriate for us to return to the courtroom immediately, that it would give the appearance that we had been frivolous in our deliberations. So we snacked on the court-provided donuts and sipped coffee while we talked animatedly about the case.

In the subsequent discussion, the proverbial scales fell from my eyes. Not only had these ladies and gentlemen, whom I'd assumed to be uncultured philistines, followed the details of the case. Some of them had picked up on angles that I, the cultured sophisticate, had missed.

I chastised myself and felt ashamed for being such a judgmental elitist for assuming that my professional career choice, coat and tie, and college education endowed me with greater common sense, insight, intellect, and reasoning ability than these others. And so I learned an important lesson that has stayed with me since, giving me valuable insights into front-line employees.

That was a long time ago. But what I learned then and what I know now is that if there is a central guiding tenet of employee communications, it's the basic dignity and respect that people in a working environment deserve from their employer, recognition for their innate intelligence and common sense.

Providing employees with relevant and helpful information

in a timely manner demonstrates respect for them as valuable individual contributors. It says that everyone here has a role to play; it says how and what one person contributes to the greater good is just as critical as anyone else in the organization.

In many business circumstances, however, people are not treated that way. Some managers are attuned more to their own rank, experience, and educational background in relation to those they regard as their subordinates and ignore the basic intelligence others have and their desire and ability to contribute. And so they talk down to them, treat them as inferior, and communicate with them accordingly.

Regardless of one's rank in the organization – CEO, vice president, or supervisor – people should always operate as though the average employee is eager and fully capable of making important contributions to the organization. He/she is intelligent and possesses common sense built over years of experience both on and off the job. Let them prove otherwise. But until then, it would be foolish to assume the opposite.

As manager or leader, you should communicate to your employees as peers, not as inferiors. Give them more information than you think they need. Recognize that people aspire to grow within organizations and learn, and that information gives them more insights into the business so they can do that on their own terms. Further, consider this counsel:

- Don't make the same mistake I made with my fellow jurors and jump to conclusions about or misjudge your employees.
- Don't assume you know what information they want or need, or what they'll do with what you give them.
- Don't presume they won't understand it or can't master its complexity. They will see it through their own lens (different

than yours) process it, and draw conclusions that may not coincide with your own.

And don't assume you know more than they do. Just because you live in the C-Suite doesn't mean you have special powers of intuition and hidden founts of knowledge. Listen to and trust your employees' insights and ideas. You might learn something.

Maybe, just maybe, you might gain new insights into how better to run the business because you trusted the unique worldview of someone you had once assumed was your lesser.

The Value of Empathy

Empathy, "the capacity to recognize or understand another's state of mind or emotion," is a powerful competitive advantage within a business organization.

Truly empathetic managers are often the best, most effective managers because they have a better, clearer understanding of how their employees operate and what motivates them, and so are able to lead a cohesive team focused on a common purpose.

The surest path to empathy is personal, first-hand experience. Many of the best managers, those with profound empathy, are those who worked their way up in their organization, which is why the wisest company founders and owners don't merely pass on the mantle of leadership to their children, but make sure they earn it.

I witnessed this first hand a number of years ago at a client company. Founded in the early-1960s, the specialty-manufacturing firm grew and thrived on the genius and drive of its founder, who had left a promising career at a global industrial company with nothing more than his ideas for a better company around a core product line and how best to produce it and deliver it to a target customer base.

As a youngster, his son Oliver often hung out with him on weekends, walking the factory floor, listening in as his dad talked shop with his employees. In high school, "Ollie," as he was known, swept floors and did other unskilled work as his summer job. Over the years, through college and post-graduate business school, he always worked full-time during the summer months in the plant doing the dirtiest jobs. It was what his father wanted. Upon graduation, his dad put him through the paces, and by the time he reached his late-thirties, Ollie had worked in every department, including billing, field sales, manufacturing, and customer service.

At the time I got to know him as a client, Ollie was head of marketing, a capable marketer with a keen understanding of his company's product lines, its markets and, especially, its customers and its customers' worlds. Ollie eventually became president and his father moved into an advisory and planning role as chairman. The company continues to thrive, and I know one of the biggest reasons for its success is the fact that its president knows his company intimately, from every perspective.

Most important, though, he knows the people who make it work. He knows from hands-on experience and personal observation what it takes to do each job. He knows the dedication, intelligence, and perseverance of the many employees who comprise the foundation of the company's success.

So it would stand to reason that a company that hires an outside senior manager or CEO with little or no first-hand knowledge of the company's inner workings and its people is asking for trouble. And the truth is, statistics show that outside CEOs and senior managers have a less than positive track record. So consider how one company approached that dilemma when they had no choice but to hire an outsider.

A friend and colleague shared with me the personal story told to him by the general manager of one of the hotels at Walt Disney World in Orlando.

This eminently qualified gentleman had been hired by Disney to run its newest hotel. He had come from a major hotel chain where he had gained a number of years' experience running several of its properties around the world.

He reported for his first day on the job impeccably dressed in suit and tie, but soon learned he had over-dressed. Handed a workman's jumpsuit and work boots, he was told that his next six months would be spent learning how the hotel operates, from the ground-up, starting with maintenance.

It was an eye-opening experience as he rotated between behind-the-scenes jobs. He unclogged toilets and helped fix balky air conditioning systems; cleaned guest rooms and changed bed linen; bussed tables in the restaurants; toted room service trays; served drinks at the bar until closing time; hauled garbage; cleaned the swimming pools; and worked the front desk and the reservations line.

In all his years in hotel management, he said, he had never fully appreciated how hard so many people worked to make the guests' stays pleasant and enjoyable experiences. Imagine what he learned about his employees' workaday lives and how he carried that empathy back with him when he assumed his real job of hotel general manager. Imagine the unique insights he gained into the inner workings of the marvelously complicated machine that such a hotel really is, the bulk of which is invisible to most guests.

The Walt Disney Company is a unique organization, focused on innovative engagement at all levels. Every employee, no matter the operation, no matter the job, is referred to as a "cast member." A concerted effort is made to maintain a positive work environment, which in turn leads to engaged employees who feel motivated, inspired and committed. Workers at all levels have the ability and control to deliver on the Disney mission statement: "To make people happy." The company's namesake and founder, Walter E. Disney, said it best:

> "*Our heritage and ideals, our code and standards—the things we live by and teach our children—are preserved or diminished by how freely we exchange ideas and feelings.*"

That's a pretty good definition of empathy, too. Don't you think?

Postscript: *After sharing this story with a good friend, she sent me a link to an article from the (Portland)* Oregonian *about a CEO's unique approach to the job. Upon being hired to lead family-owned Platt Electric, Jeff Baker spent six months incognito in the field learning first-hand how the company operated. Employees thought he was a temporary worker. He never said anything to make them think otherwise. As CEO, he managed Platt through a tough housing and real estate market without any layoffs or pay cuts. Now, he's growing the company in the face of a weak economy, stealing market share from larger competitors.*

Move Your Employees From "They" to "We"

Have you ever noticed how fickle sports fans can be? On Sunday, September 7, 2008, before the New England Patriots-Kansas City Chiefs game started, Patriot fans interviewed on TV in the parking lots were saying, "We're going to win the Super Bowl this year!"

But something terrible happened during the game, the first of the new season. In the first quarter, the Patriots' star quarterback, Tom Brady, took a solid hit to his left knee, crumpled to the turf in pain and, as we would later learn, was out for the season with torn medial and anterior cruciate ligaments (MCL and ACL). After that, fans were heard saying, "I don't think they can win this year without Brady."

How quickly things change from "We" to "They." It's not unique to New England, nor is it unique to sports. It's probably just human nature to want to associate with winners but to distance ourselves from losers, even perceived losers.

The same is true within the corporate world. In a winning company, one that is on top of its game like Facebook or Apple, the employees typically talk about the company in the first person plural. "We own the market."

But when a company is struggling, it's often, "They don't know what they're doing. They have driven this company into the ditch." In those cases, employees assume no responsibility for the decline of the company. It's someone else's fault, namely, the CEO and/or the management team.

When companies engage me to assess their internal culture and the quality of their employee communications, I will conduct numerous interviews and focus groups with managers and employees. I listen closely for that "we" and "they," whether front-line employees use the first or third person plural in reference to the company.

Frankly, in that I've usually been brought in to address perceived problems, it's more often the latter, as in, "They tried that before and it didn't work." And, "they never listen to us," etc. In cases where the companies are struggling, rarely do I hear statements like, "We're having a tough time."

It goes to my original point here. People, by nature like to be associated with winners, and tend to distance themselves from losers. But for a company facing difficult challenges, what is the tipping point between "We" and "They?" How can leaders create that sense of ownership so important through good times and bad?

While the answers to those questions are unique to each situation, the commonality to all is effective communications, which is to say, relevant information conveyed in a regular and timely manner via dialogue, discussion and debate among and between leadership, managers, supervisors and employees. Where that is the norm, the sense of ownership is far more prevalent than not and it's more likely to hear employees using "we" than "they."

People might point to a successful organization and say that developing that sense of ownership in a winning environment is easy. But I push back and ask, "Which came first, the chicken or the egg?"

More likely, the organization is successful because the environment of dialogue, discussion, and debate was well established before it began experiencing success, perhaps at the company's founding. People at all levels have a voice in the operation and, at the same time, they have a clear understanding of the company's vision and mission, as well as the strategies driving them in that direction.

Mid-course corrections in the face of competitive threats and a changing marketplace are communicated clearly and regularly. There is no such thing as a "fair weather" employee. There is little opportunity for disassociation to fester, even when the chips are down.

Of course, the professional football team metaphor is imperfect because the average fan is not an employee and has no personal stake in the outcome of the team's season, unless that fan bets on the team. For a going concern, however, the average employee indeed has a personal stake in the health and well being of his or her company – it's the source of his/her livelihood and future.

So it behooves company leadership to assure that its employees stay engaged, fully comprehending how they contribute every day to the on-going health of the business. Only then will they see that they share responsibility for its success or failure. Only then will they think of the company as their own, in the first person plural.

The Real Lessons of *"Undercover Boss"*

Waste Management, Inc., is a well-respected company that provides garbage handling, recycling, landfill management, and related services to customers and municipalities in forty-seven states. It employs about 41,000 people, with reported 2016 revenues of $13.61 billion.

In early 2010, its then-president and chief operating officer, Lawrence O'Donnell, III, or "Larry," as he preferred, became the newest TV reality show star. *Undercover Boss*, which premiered on February 7, 2010, on CBS after the Super Bowl, featured Larry's experiences on the front lines of Waste Management.

As the title suggests, the company's leader assumed a fake identity to join his employees in their daily grind so he could see what life is like in the trenches.

Larry went without shaving for a couple days, put on a green jumpsuit, and worked undercover as "Randy," tackling a range of tasks alongside his own employees who, of course, were not in on the deception. In one instance, the unknowing employee was his temporary boss, who fired "Randy." Larry/Randy got to clean portable toilets, chase and pick up loose litter at a windy landfill, sort recyclables, and ride on the back of a garbage truck on its daily route.

If you guessed that this would be like most reality shows, you were right. The unknowing employees were surprised when they learned Randy's true identity. He underwent something akin to an epiphany because of the experience.

Larry got a new view of the world from the business end of a garbage truck, apparently a cathartic occasion for him. "I didn't think I'd be having these kinds of emotional issues riding on the back of a garbage truck," he said, wiping tears away in a typical reality TV tight shot.

"I've got to change the way I go about my own job," he said, as he shed his jumpsuit and returned to his suit-and-tie uniform. Larry went back to revisit the people he had previously worked with. It was a series of *Candid Camera* moments, complete with gasps and shrieks. Naturally, he solved their problems and even promoted one of them.

One woman had griped about an absurd rule that forced employees to punch in exactly on the half-hour. Rule changed. Another woman he worked with was putting in long hours and doing several jobs, yet struggling to pay her mortgage. Larry promoted her to salaried manager with a hefty pay increase and bonus eligibility.

"All my hard work has been noticed," she said tearfully. Mortgage paid. Problem solved.

"I now have a whole new appreciation of the impact some of my decisions can have on you folks," the newly chastened president told his employees.

At the time of the premiere, the Waste Management web site was promoting the show. I'm not sure how long they kept it there. They might have come to realize the downside, and, honestly, there was a potential downside, depending on how Larry O'Donnell and his team followed through.

I can see how O'Donnell (and the other senior executives) would be excited by all this attention, but I wonder how employees not involved in the show felt when they watched it. Surely they, too, had a raft of issues that could have been quickly addressed if their CEO had spent time with them.

So would this be a win-win for the company in the long run? It would be, but only if O'Donnell and the other senior executives adopted this as a habit and made it part of their regular routine to visit the front lines.

Believe me, I'm not knocking the idea of senior level people getting out in the field among employees and experiencing personally what their people do every day. I'd like to think that this show encouraged a lot of other bosses to do the same. It's always going to be a great learning experience for both sides of the equation.

The benefits that senior executives derive from getting out on the front lines with their employees are immeasurable. Unfortunately, it's a rarity today. The higher a person gets in the organization, it seems, the less likely it is that he/she has the time to indulge in such luxuries, at least, that's what most of them say.

I contend that it most certainly is *not* a luxury and should not be seen that way. It's part of the job. But I nearly always get pushback when I suggest it to clients. The CEOs are too busy, I am told. Their calendars are filled months in advance with *important* meetings and numerous other obligations.

It's difficult to argue such a point with someone who sits atop a *Fortune 500* company with all the attendant constituencies and responsibilities. But I do some pushing back myself. Make the time, I tell them. It's your job. And it *will* make a huge difference.

It seems that too many senior executives are more attuned to the interests of Wall Street, nursing their company's image (and stock price), and spend far more time with analysts than with their own employees. They also spend a lot of time in meetings with one another in the executive suite. Big mistake. Becoming better attuned to what's going on in your own organization will do far more for your company's image (and revenues and stock price) than all the coddling of Wall Street analysts one could possibly muster.

What Leaders Can Learn By Getting Out and About

One of the surest paths to management excellence is not through books, seminars or the pursuit of an MBA, but through personal experience, getting out in the field and seeing with one's own eyes how things happen.

The previous essay here concerned the CBS television show *Undercover Boss* in which I wrote: "I'd like to think that this show will encourage a lot of other bosses to do the same. It's always going to be a great learning experience, for both sides of the equation. The benefits that senior executives derive from getting out on the front lines with their employees are immeasurable."

Apparently my wish was granted. In at least one instance, I'd like to think that the show inspired a company's senior management to get out of their offices and see for themselves what goes on out there, in a big way.

In a May 20, 2010 article, the *Boston Globe* spotlighted DHL, the international package delivery firm, and how its senior executives borrowed CBS' idea. The CEO and his senior team came to Boston for a week to work alongside their local employees, though not incognito like the TV show. Ian Clough, then the CEO for U.S. operations, was joined by several of his senior managers for the first-hand look.

Clough and the others each rode shotgun in delivery vans all day one day, going on the daily rounds with their drivers. It was a terrific learning experience, the CEO reported. As the *Globe* noted, "Clough developed the program as a way to better assess how policies enacted at upper levels of the company affect the firm's front-line workers."

Bravo!

As Clough explained, "The idea is, if the CIO or the CFO is evaluating an investment proposal for new equipment for our couriers and he's sitting in his nice warm office, he'll have [had] first-hand experience of knowing what it's like to be out on a truck in a wet and windy place like Boston."

Christine Nashick, DHL's marketing vice president and one of the participating executives, characterized the exercise as a "back-to-basics approach."

Clough introduced himself to customers at each stop and asked probing questions about their preferences in delivery services and their attitude toward DHL. People were honest, and Clough was grateful. He learned a lot, he said, and not all of it was good news.

He and his team were there to observe, not to get their hands dirty like the CEOs in *Undercover Boss*. Drivers were selected at random and paired with the executives.

The van on which Clough rode was one of the company's new hybrid trucks. Clough was interested to learn from the driver how well it performed. He was pleased to get a first-hand report from the driver, though not entirely happy to learn that the hybrids' performance left a lot to be desired.

The story mentioned that the senior executives were scheduled to go out on sales calls as well, for better insights into the customers' world, their needs, and how DHL can better support them.

I'm always heartened to learn of such out-reach activities on the part of senior executives. This kind of experience never fails to open one's eyes. It's one thing to sit in the executive suite and make decisions. It's still another to do so after having been exposed to the field where those decisions most affect the employees, the operations, and their customers.

What the *Globe* story didn't mention was the importance of the personal connections the executives make with their front-line workers. It will undoubtedly leave an indelible impression.

It will give them otherwise unattainable insights into the working environment of their employees – their daily challenges, pleasures, frustrations, and opportunities.

Decisions and discussions around capital expenditures are one thing, whether to buy new hybrid deliver vans, for instance. But now they have a better feel for the impact those decisions may have on people, perhaps the most critical aspect of any decision.

Recall what Waste Management President Larry O'Donnell said after his *Undercover Boss* experience: "I now have a whole new appreciation of the impact some of my decisions can have. . ."

Executives will have a newfound and profound perspective on how their company operates, from the bottom-up rather than from the top-down. They will have a better sense of the impact, not only of their decisions, but also of their messages and their communications.

No doubt Clough was surprised at least a few times to learn that initiatives or executive communiqués failed to reach or failed to impress the people on the ground. Let us hope, if he did get that insight, that he will rethink his messages and how he communicates them in the future.

If that were all he got out of the exercise, then it was worth the week's investment of the executives' time. Everything else was a bonus.

What Risk Aversion Communicates

"Daring ideas are like chessmen moved forward. They may be
beaten, but they may start a winning game."

Johann Wolfgang von Goethe
Poet, Philosopher
1749 – 1832

"There is more risk in not doing this than in doing it," my friend exclaimed, complaining about a frustrating situation at work. The global head of his company's IT department was balking at a major system-wide software upgrade he was urging because there was "too much security risk involved," she claimed. He was told to get back to her when *"the risk factor was zero."*

"She said we need to have zero tolerance for risk. That's impossible," my friend grumbled. "There is no such thing as zero-tolerance of risk. If you get on a plane, it could crash. Zero tolerance for risk means you'd never leave your house."

Trying to empathize and give him something to laugh about, I emailed him a timely Dilbert cartoon that ran the same week as our conversation. It concerned a recurring character named "Mordac, the Preventer of Information Services," a cautious idler who invents asinine reasons for not helping employees with their IT problems.

A lot of people in business operate like Mordac these days, when their companies are mired in the effects of a difficult economy. And not just in the IT departments. It's caution bred by fear of making the wrong choice. Yet in today's circumstances, risk is necessary if a business is to get a leg up on its competition and thrive in the long run.

Baseball Hall of Fame member Stan Musial, a former St. Louis Cardinals slugger, was one of the greatest ball players of all time. He posted a lifetime batting average of 0.331, an average that makes him the twenty-sixth best batter in all of Major League history among the thousands of non-active players. As good as that is, that average also means that for every three at-bats, he failed two times. In other words, he made two outs for every hit he got.

The better hitters like Musial maximize their at-bats, "working the count," fouling off countless pitches, wearing out the pitcher while allowing his team to get insights into the pitcher's style they can take advantage of later when the pitcher inevitably tires.

If Apple Inc. were a baseball player, it would be batting close to 1.000, and that's after taking a lot more risk than stepping in against a Major League fastball.

Within a decade of Steve Jobs rejoining the company, Apple had shaken up several businesses (desktop computing, music, and mobile communications), and created entirely new niches with its iMac, iTunes, iPod, iPhone, Apple Stores, and its iPhone apps.

In October 2009, Silicon Valley was abuzz with rumors that Apple was about to reinvent the publishing industry with some kind of electronic tablet/reader (see *"Vision Guides Product Development"* page 139) – a full six months before the actual introduction of the now-ubiquitous iPad. Based on what they'd achieved in the previous decade, I believed those rumors at the time. But even if nothing had come of it, Apple managed to "work the count" as the rumor mill kept the competition guessing, scrambling and off-balance.

Apple was willing to take risks like that, even in the context of a lousy economy, or perhaps because of it, since no one else was stretching.

Look at the copycats they competed with then – Microsoft, Dell, Samsung, Motorola, Sony, and Nokia. When was the last time one among that group took a serious risk and introduced a truly original, groundbreaking idea, on par with the hits that Apple was then producing? Have you noticed how similar the Microsoft mall stores are to Apple Stores? How about Microsoft's iPad-like "Surface?"

The problem that plagues those companies is the fear of failure and its implications, a fear that usually originates at the top. Risk-aversion is passed down the org chart. Employees mirror the way managers think and operate. If they see managers operating in a risk-averse manner, they withdraw and keep their heads down, too.

This is ultimately about communications. Leaders' and managers' behaviors and actions communicate far more than their words, and if the actions of leaders and managers demonstrate distaste for risk, they are communicating it clearly.

Risk-taking defined Steve Jobs and the Apple culture he shaped, so changing the game was (and is) not thought of as a risk at Apple. In a time of constant change, a business unwilling to create and drive change like Apple will ultimately find itself overwhelmed by the external changes forced upon it.

Back in the late 1960s, it was said that Boeing's officers and board of directors "bet the company" to develop the 747 jumbo jet. In other words, the cost of development exceeded the value of the company itself. Had the airliner been a flop, Boeing likely would have gone out of business. Now *that's* a risk. Fortunately for Boeing, the 747 has been its biggest moneymaker for the past nearly fifty years.

To Sony, Microsoft, Motorola, and others, risk seems to be anathema. They act on proven concepts. Sony and Microsoft launched their retail stores only after Apple had shown the way with its enormously successful Apple Store.

Yet the Microsoft version pales by comparison. See for yourself. Next time you are in a local mall, compare the enthusiastic, engaged crowd of customers (and I do mean *crowd*) at the Apple Store any given time of the day or week. Then, drop by and see the random visitor(s) perusing the Microsoft store, while the clerks lean on the display cases, looking bored.

Never mind looking for Sony Style stores. While Microsoft's stores division slowly added new retail outlets, Sony withdrew from the category. In early 2014, it announced it was closing 20 or its remaining 31 U.S. retail outlets.

In late summer 2009, Sony came out with a desktop PC that it described as ". . . built into an elegant widescreen LCD panel." Hmmm, looked a lot like an Apple iMac.

Since then, in early 2014, Sony withdrew from the PC market, selling its Viao PC and laptop line and brand name to Japan Industrial Partners (JIP).

Also in the summer of 2009, Motorola rolled out its Droid, a blatant iPhone imitation. And then Microsoft introduced its latest "game changer," Windows 7 (yet another Mac OS copy).

Look, businesses are founded by people who take risks – often huge risks – with their own personal savings and reputations. The irony is that once those companies become successful, grow, add people, and go public, risk-taking usually becomes an increasingly scary concept.

Management moves from quarter to quarter, seeking to sustain a certain level of revenue growth, usually by doing the same things, adding little flourishes to make the old seem new. Few will take the big gamble to reinvent themselves or an entire industry the way Boeing did with the 747 in the 1960s or Apple did during Steve Jobs' second tenure there.

Meanwhile, as my friend noted, his department's best people left, running from the overly cautious culture. (Six months after our conversation, he left, too.) The better people in any organization want to be challenged. They want to be able to take risks, to try their new ideas. They don't want to have to keep their heads down and hide in cubicles.

American businessman and oilman T. Boone Pickens once said, "Be willing to make decisions. That's the most important quality of a good leader. Don't fall victim to what I call the 'ready-aim-aim-aim syndrome.' You must be willing to fire."

At its heart, that's what risk is all about – people willing to make decisions, to say "yes" to risk. Many of us have experienced the corporate environment where "everyone has the power to say 'no,' but no one has the authority to say 'yes'." This is a time for leaders to say "yes," to encourage their people to pursue cutting edge ideas, risks that might fail, but that might also succeed and reinvent their companies, opening new realms of opportunity.

Organizational Vision

"If you want to build a ship, don't drum up the men
to gather wood, divide the work, and give orders.
Instead, teach them to yearn for the vast and endless sea."

Antoine de Saint-Exupéry
Author, Aviator
1900 – 1944

Build on Your Foundation of Heritage

In the 1830s, a nineteen-year-old Vermont blacksmith resettled in Grand Detour, IL, to establish himself in his trade. In the course of his work, he perfected a tool that would revolutionize agriculture, literally open the American Prairie, and lead to the settlement of the West.

John Deere's 1837 singular invention was the steel plow, "The plow that broke the plains." He formed his eponymous company in Moline, IL, to manufacture and sell it and related farm equipment. The company grew rapidly to become what it is today, the world's largest farm and construction equipment company.

Imagine a line worker at a Deere manufacturing facility today. I wonder how well that hourly employee knows the origins of his company and, if so, what it means to him. If I were a manager there, I would use two recurring quotes in my internal communications.

The first would be the anchor phrase: "The plow that broke the plains." It's the foundation on which the company was built, the pride of its founder, and the basis for its launch and initial success.

The second quote would be from John Deere himself. From the beginning, he placed special emphasis on quality and personalized it. He said, "I will never put my name on a product that does not have in it the best that is in me."

That attitude, no doubt, is what drove the company to its long-term success and what has sustained it through good times and bad. That quote should permeate the company's internal communications. Every employee should embrace the attitude it evokes with the full appreciation of the "John Deere" nameplate on every product that rolls out its doors; an attitude that says the individual employee's own reputation is also at stake with each product.

Deere's face to the public, to its customer audience, is: "Nothing runs like a Deere," a clever and enduring pun that evokes reliability. That's fine and that's how it should position itself in the marketplace.

But for the internal audience, there is incalculable worth in connecting everyone's work to the founder's unequivocal attitude toward quality, in connecting everyone to that same fundamental value and the company's heritage of that simple steel plow.

Numerous other companies can brag of a deep legacy like Deere's. General Electric was founded on Thomas Edison's invention of the electric light bulb and related electrical generation and distribution equipment, as well as his unparalleled work ethic. While Edison's legend may have faded in his home country and within GE itself, the engineering culture that dominates Japanese business reveres Edison's memory to this day and his connection to GE.

IBM was built on the fertile mind and entrepreneurial genius of Thomas J. Watson. The Walt Disney Company was shaped on the imaginative genius of its namesake and his alter ego, Mickey Mouse, who remains the ever-cheerful mascot of the global enterprise.

McDonald's was a local San Bernardino, CA, hamburger stand until Ray Kroc bought it and turned it into the world's largest fast food eatery based on his "QSVC" principles: quality, service, value and cleanliness. Hewlett-Packard Development Company has enshrined the Palo Alto garage where, in 1939, William Hewlett and

David Packard developed the company's first product, an audio oscillator.

Most every company has a remarkable founding history, too, no matter how young or old it may be. Twenty-year-old entrepreneurs are dropping out of college every day, it seems, in a rush to bring their cutting-edge ideas to life. If their ideas are solid, and if they work hard enough and are determined, their companies could become tomorrow's IBM, General Electric or McDonald's.

Everyone, it seems, is familiar with the stories of Mark Zuckerberg dropping out of Harvard to found Facebook, how Sergey Brin and Larry Page left Stanford and started Google.

A friend told me the exciting story of his company, a new business just getting off the ground on the basis of his and his business partners' compelling original idea. As he explained the business and its potential in greater detail, I jealously wished I had thought of it. His company, too, will become great one day if he and his partners are persistent and work hard. I'm sure they will.

As my friend and his partners work those long hours, suffer disappointments amidst their celebrations and milestones over time, they will simultaneously be creating their company's heritage that will give it meaning for years to come, long after they've retired.

All companies have histories, or "stories." By telling and retelling these histories, people can connect to, feel, and understand the mission, values and passion that have built, grown, and sustained their companies.

Corporate brands reflect their companies' heritages. With successful brands, the pride and emotion they generate are shared with new employees like family heirlooms passed along from one generation to the next. In a sports context, devoted fans honor the memories of their teams' greatest stars and seasons of victory.

The New York Yankees provide an excellent example, with their century worth of countless all-stars, and twenty-seven World Series championships. Green Bay Packers fans readily connect their latest Super Bowl championship to the era of Vince Lombardi and Bart Starr, when they were equally invincible. Boston Celtics fans reminisce about Bill Russell, Larry Bird, Bob Cousey, Bill Havlicek, and the team's seventeen NBA championships as they root for the latest edition of their Celtics.

In a time of radical shifts, as companies endeavor to respond and adapt to the evolving marketplace, a company's heritage provides a valuable foundation upon which to build for the future, a touchstone to guide the people through times of uncertainty and difficulty.

Sometimes it's a person and his/her performance or innovation, like John Deere, Babe Ruth, Thomas Edison, Bill Russell, or Walt Disney. Sometimes it's an event or point in time that gave birth to the company or marked a significant turning point, such as the break-up of AT&T in the early 1980s that resulted in the creation of eight new regional phone companies. Maybe it's like the 1982 Tylenol poisoning case that permanently changed the way that Johnson & Johnson engaged its customers.

Every company must hang onto and tap into its founding vision and its heritage so that employees can connect to its essential meaning. Doing so gives employees a stronger sense of belonging, of continuity with something larger than themselves. It adds significance and value to everything they do and their contributions to the larger whole. It connects what they do to all that has been done in the company's name over its entire history.

How Steve Jobs Drove Apple's Vision

I have owned, used and trusted Apple computers since 1984 when I bought my first computer, an Apple IIc. Since buying my first Macintosh in 1989, I've never used another brand and cannot imagine why I would ever buy a Windows-based machine. I now use an iMac desktop computer, carry an iPhone in my pocket, and tote a MacBook Air in my briefcase.

Knowing my bias and interest, a friend alerted me to a book he was certain I'd appreciate. He was right. The book, "Inside Steve's Brain," by Leander Kahney, news editor for Wired.com, is about the way the late Steve Jobs thought, how he operated, how he built Apple, his successes (and mistakes), his stunning insights and innovations, and his decidedly unique approach to the world.

But it's a lot more than that. It's a business book full of valuable ideas and insights into one of the hottest companies of our time. In addition to all that the reader will learn implicitly, the book makes it easy by concluding each chapter with a helpful summary list of "Lessons from Steve."

Jobs' success was not a simple formula and thus deserves a book-length exploration that a blog entry or simple book review cannot fulfill. But here's the crux: Steve Jobs found the best people, attracted them and, once he had them on board, allowed them the freedom to do their best work. At the same time, he demanded perfection. He didn't suffer fools gladly. Known for his abrasiveness and impatience, Jobs divided the world in half, into "geniuses and bozos." He weeded out the bozos from his company, should any somehow sneak in.

Collaboration was central to how Jobs operated. The book explains that at Apple, the design, engineering, manufacturing, and marketing teams work side-by-side throughout the development process so there is little opportunity for miscommunication. Not so at other companies.

Jobs compared the approach to "seeing a cool prototype car at a car show, but when the production model appears four years later, it sucks. And you go, what happened? They had it! They had it in the palm of their hands! They grabbed defeat from the jaws of victory! . . . What happened was, the designers came up with this really great idea. Then they take it to the engineers and the engineers go, 'Nah, we can't do that. That's impossible.' And so it gets a lot worse. Then they take it to the manufacturing people and they go, 'We can't build that!' And it gets a lot worse."

Pixar, Jobs' other baby, is discussed within the context of how he put together teams of talented people and allowed them to thrive. The book contrasts Pixar's way of doing things to the typical Hollywood approach. Pixar, by the way, was not then headquartered in Hollywood nor the Los Angeles area, but in Emeryville in the East Bay, south of Berkeley at the eastern terminus of the Bay Bridge.

In Hollywood, every one is a free agent – directors, writers, actors, etc. The deal is pitched pulling together the various talents. As Kahney notes, the people are finally working together smoothly about the time the filming is wrapped up. Pixar operates on the opposite model.

At Pixar, the directors, screenwriters, and crew are all salaried employees with hefty stock option grants. Core teams of writers, directors, and animators work together on films, all as company employees. In Hollywood, studios fund story ideas, the famous Hollywood pitch.

Instead of funding pitches and story ideas, Pixar funds the career development of its employees. At the heart of the company's "people investment" culture is Pixar University, an on-the-job training program that offers hundreds of courses in art, animation, and filmmaking. All of Pixar's employees are encouraged to take classes in whatever they like, whether it's relevant to their job or not. (Note: this was originally written before Disney acquired Pixar and while Jobs was still alive, so some of these systems may have fallen by the wayside.)

It's no surprise that Jobs earned remarkable allegiance from his people. We can see the results for ourselves in the great products those people create and the sales of those products. I'd read before the sales statistics for the iPod, but the book reiterates them, and they're worth repeating here as a demonstration of the success of the Apple model.

According to the most recent sales statistics cited in the book, the company sold 275 million iPods, and more than forty-two million iPhones through the first quarter of 2010. It says that some analysts think the iPod could become a contender for the biggest consumer electronics hit of all time. The current record holder is the Sony Walkman, which sold 350 million units during its fifteen-year reign in the 1980s and early 1990s.

Incidentally, Kahney writes at length contrasting Apple and Sony and how they develop and market new products. What I find most telling is Apple's (and Jobs') near-total focus on the customer experience (in contrast to companies like Sony). While most companies just make products, Apple's approach reflects the title of a 2005 Forrester Research study: "Sell the digital experiences, not products," which the book cites. Chapter 6, on Innovation, concludes with the following "Lessons from Steve":

- Don't lose sight of the customer. The [Macintosh] Cube bombed because it was built for designers, not customers.

- Study the market and the industry. Jobs is constantly looking to see what new technologies are coming down the pike.

- Don't consciously think about innovation. Systemizing innovation is like watching Michael Dell dance. Painful.

- Concentrate on products. Products are the gravitational force that pulls it all together.

- Remember that motives make a difference. Concentrate on great products, not becoming the biggest or the richest.

- Steal. Be shameless about stealing other people's great ideas.

- Connect. For Jobs, creativity is simply connecting things.

- Study. Jobs is a keen student of art, design and architecture. He even runs around parking lots looking at Mercedes.

- Be flexible. Jobs dropped a lot of long-cherished traditions that made Apple special and kept it small.

- Burn the boats. Jobs killed the most popular iPod [the Mini] to make room for a new thinner model. Burn the boats, and you must stand and fight.

- Prototype. Even Apple's stores were developed like every other product . . . prototyped, edited, refined.

- Ask customers. The popular Genius Bar idea came from customers.

If that's not a formula for success in any field, then I don't know what is.

The Dangers of Resting on Your Reputation

Whether your business involves medical devices, automobiles, property management, insurance, professional services or fine dining, one core rule applies: If your front-line people, those who interact with your customers, are out of synch with your vision of the business, then trouble is brewing.

The thought occurred to me recently while I was out dining with friends at a fine restaurant. No matter what's being bought, if the prices are steep, then so are customer expectations. And our hosts' expectations that night were not met, for reasons too complex and numerous to go into here.

Complaints were voiced and the manager spoken to. But the bottom line is, neither our hosts nor any of their guests are likely to return. It's also likely that neither they nor we will speak well of this establishment to friends.

That kind of experience tends to discourage repeat business. People go once and don't come back. These customers' dissatisfaction is usually shared with others via word-of-mouth, but rarely with the restaurant owner. So when the restaurant owner sees an increasing number of empty seats night after night and eventually goes out of business, he wonders why. Was it the food? The ambience? The service?

On the flip side, visit a pricey restaurant that's thriving, where it's difficult to get a reservation, and you'll likely also see the owner/manager in the dining room wandering around visiting with patrons to get a sense of their satisfaction with the food and service. He/she will observe the pace in the kitchen while making sure dishes are being prepared to the restaurant's standards and make certain that the servers are attentive, responsive, and courteous.

The owner/manager sees each meal served as an extension of him/herself and is dissatisfied with anything that falls short, lest it reflect poorly on him/her. Over time, with repeat business and positive word-of-mouth, the restaurant thrives, building more repeat business, a loyal clientele, and a solid reputation for good food, a pleasant ambience, and superb service.

But beware the restaurant that dines out on its reputation without consistent, on-going vigilance to assure that its reputation stays earned. In a people-intensive business like a restaurant that takes its eye off the ball, the flaws are soon on display for all to see, especially the customers.

While the same truths apply to any business with employees, it's often not readily apparent to a senior manager in a larger enterprise.

For instance, a national sales organization with a couple dozen field sales people scattered around the country is a different proposition altogether than a single restaurant where the person in charge can get real time, first-hand insights into what's working and what isn't, and customer input.

Twenty-four different people, on the road every day without day-to-day organizational contact or a guiding vision, can soon become mavericks, each operating independently with their own unique sense of what the company stands for. Pretty soon, the company stands for little or nothing.

It also applies to retail businesses built on a founding vision of someone like John Mackey of Whole Foods, Howard Schultz of

Starbucks, or the late Sam Walton of Wal-Mart. Larger businesses like these grew from small beginnings and thrived because of the ability of their owners/founders to communicate their vision effectively and consistently to employees and managers as the business expanded and opened new franchises.

To Sam Walton (as well as the founders of other such organizations), vision was what he saw that Wal-Mart could become if he and his people tended to what defined them.

I once read a comment attributed to a Wal-Mart board member. When the board deadlocks on a difficult decision, he said, the fallback position is often to ask, "What would Sam do?" (This is in spite of the fact that Walton passed away in 1992.) It's a standard question that most managers and employees also ask to reconnect to that foundation of Sam Walton's vision. In that way and others, Wal-Mart has successfully maintained its focus on its founder's personal imprint, his unstinting focus on the customer.

On the other hand, a large business with an international footprint can coast for a long time on the inertia of a reputation it built over decades. Consider, for example, General Motors, which was on a path toward failure for at least ten years, some would argue longer. The ultimate bankruptcy of an organization like GM is far slower than a single restaurant or small business. But the causes and effect are the same.

A business is bound to fail if its managers and leaders take their eyes off the ball, dining out on their reputation without constantly refreshing it by keeping their people engaged in the business' core vision.

Communicate Your Vision Effectively

A business is launched on a core vision, a driving purpose, likely the brainchild of its founder. Initial success comes with the founder's ability to make that vision a reality through hard work and a relentless focus on that ultimate destination.

As the business grows and adds employees, its continued success and growth is dependent on how well the founder is able to impart his/her vision to the new people so that they, too, share that founding vision and are able to act on it through effective implementation of the company's strategy.

Regardless of whether the business is only a decade old, like Google, or is more than one hundred years old, like General Electric, the same holds true: the continued success of that company is dependent on employees comprehending and acting on its vision.

Visions evolve and adapt to changing circumstances, such as recessionary or expanding economies, shrinking or growing markets, shifts in customer needs and tastes, etc. And so, too, must the company help employees evolve and adapt. Even the one-hundred-year-old company can stay as fresh, focused and competitive as a new start-up if it keeps its people engaged in the evolving vision.

This is a round-about way of getting to my point – the importance of also engaging employee communications consultants in the business' core vision, as well as its strategy, the needs and desires of its customers, and the changing dynamics of its markets. A consultant comes into an organization for a discrete period of time, provides advice and counsel, sometimes helps develop and execute a strategy, and then leaves. The ideal is where the outsider can be immersed fully in the business, gaining understanding of and a full appreciation for its products and services, markets, customers, and unique challenges.

From the perspective of communications consultants, those are the best assignments in terms of gaining personal satisfaction from the work, and, most important, in terms of their ability to provide helpful and valuable counsel. Regardless of the product or service a client company sells, the consultant's ability to appreciate fully the circumstances in which that company operates provides valuable insights into the struggles and challenges, risks, victories, and mistakes that comprise the daily experience of employees.

Their communications counsel is far more insightful and meaningful when they know that experience intimately as opposed to those cases where they do not have that advantage.

Kept at arms' length from the business and given little opportunity to be as immersed as they need to be, the communications counsel provided is necessarily superficial and incomplete. Most of the work in these cases tends to be rote, tactical, and reactive. Further, there is little pleasure in the assignment. It's more of a struggle, where they're not allowed to do their best work.

There's often no way of knowing ahead of time into which category a new client will fall. There might be some early tip-offs. When the new client talks about "catching a speeding train" (a metaphor a client once used with me), employs a similar allusion, or says there's no time "for the luxury" of immersing ourselves in the business, it's likely it will be a tactically intensive assignment with little chance to connect personally or provide insightful strategic counsel. When the assignments conclude, the client is not likely to be satisfied. I remember one such case. We had spent nearly a year chasing that speeding train, forced to be reactive and tactical in our communications work, with few opportunities provided to immerse ourselves in the company's culture, to learn how employees operated, and how they preferred to get information, and then to develop an effective communications strategy. As we wound down the assignment, the client complained that we hadn't provided much strategic guidance. *Hello? Come again? What did you expect?*

Conversely, a client open to the notion of allowing the communications consultant a full engagement in the business, able to talk with employees prior to commencing the assignment, is going to get full value for the investment because the outside counsel will gain important awareness and understanding of the employees' environment, challenges, and a personal connection to the business.

Most companies employ full-time communications managers. Outside communications consultants should be brought in not to replicate or supplement their work, but rather to provide the outsider's perspective that the insider cannot possibly have. That's where the full value comes in – being able to understand fully the business' vision, mission, strategy, challenges, markets, and customer demands, and then translate that into meaningful communications strategies and messages to help keep employees engaged in the business.

The deeper, first-hand appreciation for the personal investments that each employee makes in the job is the key to engaging the employees in dialogue and discussion, and being better equipped to shape the right messages to assure that employees are getting the right information, insights, and knowledge at the right time, through the right channels for maximum effect.

And if that's what the client is paying for, why erect barriers?

How *The Wall Street Journal* **Approached the iPad**

As both a print and online subscriber to *The Wall Street Journal*, I am occasionally asked to participate in their online surveys. Often, these are done for the benefit of advertisers, to get a read on how well their messages are getting through.

Other times, the surveys are more interesting and concern the *Journal* itself, what kinds of stories I like, what needs to get more coverage (or less), and other issues along those lines. But a February 2010 survey piqued my interest and, in my mind, showed how on-the-ball the people at the *Journal* are.

At the time, *The Wall Street Journal* was available in three different media, conventional newsprint, the WSJ.com web site, and the WSJ iPhone app. The latter is a nifty little app that includes breaking news (of all kinds, not just business news), stock market quotes, video, and even WSJ Radio. It can be customized to suit the whims of the user. But the limitations of the small screen format restricted their inventiveness.

The survey I completed asked a series of questions about how I use their web site versus their print edition versus the iPhone app. How does their iPhone app compare to other news apps, including *The New York Times*, FOX News, and the AP's "Mobile News?" What is better about one versus the others, and why? Do I ever click on advertisers' banners? Etcetera.

Then they wanted to know whether I was planning to buy an Apple iPad within the next six months. Mind you, this was more than a month before the device would be available in the Apple Stores. At that time, I was undecided on the question, but because I was curious why they were asking, I checked the "yes" box. Therein ensued several specific questions about how I expected to use the iPad, whether to read books, magazines, and newspapers; play games; watch movies; send and receive email; listen to music, etc.

Would I welcome a special iPad WSJ application? [Yes.] Would I be willing to pay extra for it? [No, I wouldn't.] Would banner ads be okay? [Sure. Why not?] And how would I prefer the app to be formatted, like the iPhone app or like the print edition? [Print.]

The survey was striking because it showed how Dow-Jones was continuing to stay ahead of the technology curve. Remember, they were the first major player with a subscription-only web site, and, at the time, they were one of the few (if not the only) media companies making money on its web site subscriptions.

One of their chief competitors, *The New York Times*, has long been struggling with "monetizing" its web site, an effort that has been marked with fits and starts the past few years. For a time, the *Times* tried to charge for access to certain columnists. That failed, and the experiment ended.

At heart, the poll about the iPad once again demonstrated why *The Wall Street Journal* (and Dow-Jones) is about the only truly successful and dynamic media company today. While other newspapers lose subscribers and advertisers, and grand old names in the business fall by the wayside, the *Journal* continues to add subscribers and advertisers and grow. It's understandable why News Corp. was willing to pay a premium when it bought Dow-Jones.

Here was a product, the iPad, that wouldn't even be available for another month and the *Journal* was trying to figure out how best to maximize the new medium's potential by asking its customers directly. Everyone fully expected that the iPad would succeed – as indeed it has, just as the iPod, iTunes, and the iPhone did.

Businesses like Dow-Jones would be wise to hitch a ride on that anticipated success, to maintain that sense of curiosity about new and evolving technologies and their implications on their businesses.

Vision Guides Product Development

Imagine being a buggy whip maker one hundred years ago. Orders are falling year after year because your customers are starting to buy automobiles and, each year, fewer of them need buggy whips. What is the solution to your drop in sales, revenue, and profits?

Do you cut costs? Create a better buggy whip? Do you shut down operations? Or do you diversify into a new field, say, supplying the burgeoning auto industry with something it needs that suits your manufacturing capabilities?

Answering that question now with 20/20 hindsight is easy. But flash forward to now. A lot of businesses are facing similar dilemmas today. Circumstances demand that they respond quickly with answers to questions they haven't yet learned to ask.

I got to thinking about this back in October 2009 when the rumor mill was rife with speculations that Apple Inc. was close to introducing a "tablet." Brian Lam, who writes an astute technology blog called *Gizmodo*, broke the news in early October 2009 in a detailed entry full of quotes from unnamed "inside" sources.

Whereas, Amazon.com's Kindle tablet at the time was fairly static with limited capabilities, the Apple tablet sounded like it would be much more dynamic, more interactive and, most importantly, would seek to redefine print media. This would not be a Kindle copycat. Based on how Apple reinvented the music industry with iTunes and the iPod, my bet then was that they would do the same thing to print media. As it has played out, it appears I was right.

Think about the state of newspapers and magazines today. Those that haven't already folded are moving in that direction. *The Rocky Mountain News*, one of the nation's oldest papers, shut down in March 2009. In October 2009, Condé Nast announced that the venerable old cooking magazine, *Gourmet*, would soon cease publication.

According to the October 7, 2009 *Boston Globe*, Platinum Equity, a Beverly Hills buy-out firm, "broke into the news business last May, acquiring the *San Diego Union-Tribune* for a reported $50 million . . . [T]he firm's executives have turned to a familiar playbook, laying off twenty-eight percent of the paper's employees, or 304 people, including seven of its top nine executives." Platinum, as the story notes, was rumored to be interested in buying the *Globe*. It's no wonder the *Globe* writer was interested, and likely anxious.

Few newspapers and magazines were making a profit those days, and nearly all were laying people off, reducing the news hole, and examining every corner of their operations for potential savings. (And what little news hole they have left is often filled with wire copy instead of stories written by their own staffs.) In short, the managers of this modern day buggy whip industry were trying to stay in business by producing their buggy whips more cheaply.

Apple was telling them that there was another way to look at this. According to the October 2009 *Gizmodo* report, Apple had been holding surreptitious meetings with newspaper publishers like *The New York Times*, textbook publishers like McGraw-Hill, and magazine publishers like Condé Nast. Lam wrote:

> *"The eventual goal is to have publishers create hybridized content that draws from audio, video, interactive graphics in books, magazines, and newspapers, where paper layouts would be static.*

And with release dates for Microsoft's Courier set to be quite far away and Kindle stuck with relatively static e-ink, it appears Apple is moving toward a pole position in distribution of this next-generation print content."

Recall the introduction of iTunes in January 2001, which many people forget preceded the introduction of the iPod. iTunes was a new feature of the latest iteration of Apple's Macintosh operating system, Mac OS X. Mac fans loved it immediately (myself included), uploading their music CD collections, supplemented by music they bought from the new iTunes Store, which enabled them to listen to music at their desks or Mac laptops.

So when the iPod came out ten months later, Mac owners were predisposed to buy iPods. They already were familiar with its software architecture and had loaded onto their computers most of the music they would listen to on a portable device, hence, the phenomenal sales right out of the starting gate. (When the iPod was later made compatible with Windows machines, sales soared.)

Brian Lam said in *Gizmodo* that Apple was talking to publishers about putting their static content on iTunes for downloading onto customers' iPhone and iPod Touch. If you have one of those devices, you know that their two-by-three-inch screen is good for a lot of things, but probably not textbooks and such.

Sometime in the near future, Apple would roll out the new hardware that would – guess what! – perfectly suit these content providers, enabling them to grow and monetize their offerings. Indeed, Apple did introduce its iPad six months after the rumor mill started churning. It was yet another reinventing of Apple in an entirely new medium, regaining their audiences by engaging them differently.

While some in the publishing industry likely bristled at Apple's intrusion into their business, as had the music industry moguls over iTunes, the smart ones will climb aboard and move forward with this new technology. [See *"How* The Wall Street Journal *Approached the iPad,* page 136.] From the vantage point of early 2010, it was difficult for us to envision where this new technology might take us, just as we couldn't have foreseen where the iPod would go and what it would mean to professional musicians, the music industry, and music aficionados.

The answer may lie in the key phrase in the *Gizmodo* blog—"hybridized content." Business reporter Dan Lyons, who at the time moonlighted as the "Fake Steve Jobs" in his satirical yet perceptive blog, *The Secret Diary of Steve Jobs,* insightfully explained, as Steve Jobs' alter ego, the implications of an Apple tablet:

> *"[N]ew technology spawns new ways to tell stories. That's the really exciting thing here. Not the tablet itself, but what it means for news, for entertainment, for literature . . . There is no point in moving to digital readers if we're just going to do what we did on paper. . . We're talking about an entirely new way to convey information, one that incorporates dynamic elements (audio, video) with static elements (text, photos) plus the ability for the 'audience' to become content creators, not just content consumers."*

For satire, that insight was pretty darn prescient.

If I had been a reporter at a major metro daily, losing sleep, anxious for my job and paycheck, and I had read that blog entry, I would have been comforted and seen the impending development as a ray of hope. It would certainly look more promising than the slashing and burning going on in that business now.

Our Workaday Lives

"The more I want to get something done, the less I call it work."

Richard Bach
Author
1936 –

At the Movies:
What *"Up in the Air"* Tells Us About Our Work

We never know what we have until we lose it, especially our job. That's the underlying message I took from a film I recently saw.

Up In The Air, starring George Clooney, is a well-crafted, thought-provoking story of a man whose profession is to be the bearer of bad news, delivering those blasé, insipid words that carry such weight and terror to the recipient: *"We're gonna have to let you go."*

Spoiler Alert! If you haven't seen this film and intend to, you may not want to read what follows.

Ryan Bingham (Clooney) is the hired gun who casually goes about his business as the most skillful executioner from "CTC" (Career Transition Counseling), always in transit to the site of the next layoffs.

Having borne the task myself of letting people go, as well as being on the receiving end, I can attest to the unpleasantness of the moment. It's understandable, then, that a company might want to hire an outside firm to do its dirty work.

I cannot say whether such firms exist. And I'm not sure where you would go to find such a service. But for the sake of the storyline, let's assume they're out there, thriving in the 9.9-plus percent unemployment prevalent at the time of the film's release. Indeed, Craig Gregory (played by Jason Bateman), president of the fictitious CTC, is excited. *"The economic downturn has created a wonderful opportunity for the firm,*" he announces with a smile at a staff meeting.

The film offers unsurprising glimpses into the pain and loss that people feel when their livelihoods are taken from them. Their experiences are made much worse because they happen in face-to-face meetings with this hard-hearted man who isn't even their boss, whom they'd never laid eyes on before, and will likely never see again.

It's only later that we come to realize that Bingham in fact has a humane side; that he truly does understand and empathize with his victims, even if his prepared patter betrays a hard-shelled, unfeeling approach to his job. His new partner, Natalie Keener (Anna Kendrick), is a self-assured young college graduate who doesn't sense his empathy through his apparently canned spiel.

It's only later when an employee is laid off and threatens suicide that the young assistant is taken off her stride. And when they later learn the suicide threat has been acted on, she quits, unable to bear the real life pain that her work has come to represent.

Bingham, too, is affected by the suicide, but more so by his gradual realization of the larger picture of his chosen field. The film's title has both literal and figurative meanings. The newly unemployed find themselves up in the air, untethered to the reality of the jobs that had defined their lives. Also, "up in the air" quite literally describes Bingham's life of being always on the road, living in the fast lane, flying between assignments, racking up frequent flyer miles toward his nirvana of ten million miles. Bingham blandly observes, "*Last year I spent 322 days on the road, which meant I spent forty-three miserable days at home*" in Omaha.

It's toward the end that we begin to understand that the haughty, self-confident central character is himself up in the air about everything—his life, his career, his estranged family, and his torrid, cynical affair with Alex Goran (Vera Farmiga), another road warrior.

Bingham comes to see the hollowness of his quest for the supreme ten million mile club when he finally achieves it. He knows it's a metaphor for his life. As they celebrate mid-flight, the pilot asks where he's from. *"Here,"* he replies, nodding to the plane's interior. In the course of the story, we also get a realistic look at the normal human reactions to the news of losing one's job. Tears, anger, disbelief, and argumentativeness—it's all there. As Bingham says, *"We're here to make limbo tolerable."*

This is an allegorical tale of the conflict between the romantic fantasy of air travel and fancy hotels versus the reality of delays and lost luggage, set in parallel to the conflict between the ideal of a fulfilling career and the real possibility of job loss.

Bingham's words seek to console the jobless clients, to assure them that this might be the break they were waiting for, that they were stuck in a rut. He tells one older man unconvincingly that it might be his chance to become a chef, to fulfill that dream he once had.

In the end, it's a depressing tale, especially in the context of today's uncertainties around employment and job security. People today are happy to be able simply to take home a paycheck. Few can afford to bemoan their philosophical misgivings at the stress and drudgery.

Many fantasize about what they'd rather be doing. We look enviously on those who had the youthful forethought, wisdom, courage and drive to aim for and stick to a long-term career goal. They are now comfortably ensconced in early retirement, no doubt traveling at leisure on the same planes as the road warriors like Bingham that continue their Sisyphean haunting of the skies.

Be Present in the Moment

Imagine this scene. You're deep in a conversation with a colleague in his office. You're both totally focused on dealing with an issue, when suddenly someone barges in and interrupts, demanding your immediate attention.

Do you engage the interrupter, ignoring the person you were previously talking to? Of course you don't. That would be considered rude. In fact, most civilized people do not interrupt in that manner, unless it's to convey some urgent news, like, *"The building is on fire and we have to evacuate!"*

So why do we allow incoming emails on our smartphones to interrupt what we are doing in the moment, particularly when that moment involves other people?

I remember a client meeting I attended a number of years ago before the arrival of the BlackBerry (later, the iPhone) enabled email portability. It involved key personnel for the business unit's monthly update. Participants represented all aspects of the operation.

The national sales manager walked in carrying his over-flowing in-box and placed a wastebasket next to his chair before sitting. He then proceeded to go through the entire in-box, disposing of this document or that, penciling notes on another, and so on throughout the meeting.

I was appalled by his rudeness, and further by the fact that the man running the meeting, his boss, allowed it to continue. But isn't that the equivalent of people in a meeting reading and sending emails on their smartphones? In my mind, there is no difference. A smartphone is just subtler than a hulking in-box.

Similarly, what do we make of a boss who postpones discussion of an urgent topic with us until he next sees us, then, when we finally get to sit with him, he spends the entire meeting staring at his iPhone, scanning a series of messages and answering some of them? Is he more focused on us and the issue at hand, or the extraneous email that pops up on his iPhone? Will his response fully reflect the information we've given him? I doubt it.

I'm reminded of the 1971 book "Be Here Now" by Baba Ram Dass, née Richard Alpert, about his experience in Eastern religions and his discovery of the value of being present in the moment. It's a core truth not just for those seeking spiritual enlightenment but in business as well. It's the imperative of being here now, being present in the moment for ourselves and, more to the point, for the people we work and live with.

If organizational communications are to be effective, everyone must connect completely, not halfway. Persistent use of smartphones when we should be engaging other people is, in my mind, halfway, probably less.

Some people like to brag about their ability to "multi-task" and still be engaged. I disagree. It's not humanly possible. One person may think he's able to do two or three things at once, but he is not doing them as well as he might if he were focused on just one of them. It's like a flying car; it can fly through the air and it can traverse the asphalt. But it's lousy airplane and a dreadful road machine.

These same people insist that they can follow the thread of the meeting while perusing their smartphone. I beg to differ. While they may glean the gist of what's being said, they will miss the nuances and subtleties of the discussion. And that's to say nothing of the disrespect they show their colleagues as their attention focuses elsewhere.

It's a continuing frustration as a communications consultant to have to deal with this on-going rudeness, not so much for the fact that I feel it's a sign of disrespect as it is an indication of someone's inability to focus, to be present in the moment with me and other colleagues and fully participate in the issues at hand, engaging us and the topic completely.

A manager's inability or lack of desire to control the extraneous use of smartphones in meetings is a manager that likely has other issues impeding communications and, therefore, his/her ability to operate effectively as a manager.

The June 22, 2009, edition of *The New York Times* ran an article titled "Mind Your BlackBerry or Mind Your Manners," about the ubiquity of BlackBerrys, iPhones and the like in our modern business world and people's propensity to focus on them at all times.

The article (thankfully) noted, "A spirited debate about etiquette has broken out. Traditionalists say the use of BlackBerrys and iPhones in meetings is as gauche as ordering out for pizza. Techno-evangelists insist that to ignore real-time text messages in a need-it-yesterday world is to invite peril."

I side with the traditionalists. As this story added, increasingly, organizations and managers are demanding a "BlackBerrys off" policy for their meetings. When he was CEO of Ford Motor Company, Alan Mulally ordered his direct reports to turn off their BlackBerrys for his weekly team meeting. And I'm sure he's not alone in that edict.

I heartily endorse that approach, counsel my clients similarly, and hope it will spread with the same speed as did the "No Smoking" in meetings policy in the 1980s and 1990s.

Just as cigarette smoke once polluted the atmosphere of business meetings, so too do smartphones now. Perhaps we can hope for the day when the use of smartphones in meetings will go the way of cigarette smoking in meetings so that we can all *Be Here Now*, free of the metaphorical haze of electronic communications.

Why Passion Equals Success

What kinds of people do we most envy? I'm not talking about envy in the negative, covetous sense of desiring someone else's luxurious car or palatial home. This isn't about yearning for material wealth. This is a more positive envy, about admiring the people who are doing what they want, whose profession is their passion.

Think of it another way. What are the qualities of your ideal manager, someone you'd be eager to work for and with?

A friend of mine, whom I'll call Tim, is such a person, someone I've long admired and who I enjoy being with. Early in his career, he aimed high. He chose his path, the business he wanted to be in, and identified the appropriate milestones he needed to hit along the way to reach his goal. It was never easy. He built his company from scratch, putting in long hours for many years, while taking a lot of risks along the way to achieve it. But he has arrived.

The business Tim owns is thriving today. Over the years, he hired and cultivated competent managers, which ultimately freed him from much of the day-to-day hassles of running the business, while giving him more free time. He has assumed a senior advisory role in his company, which allows him time to travel extensively and play lots of golf. Once, I asked what exactly it is that he does, now that he has achieved his intended goal.

"I manage the life of Tim," he replied, with a big grin. What a perfect reply. While on its face it seems self-centered, in fact, it says in six simple words what we all crave at our core . . . the sense of *I'm in control of my life.*

In the end, that's what we envy most about the people we deem worthy of our respect – they are in control of their lives. How they spend their time and what they choose to do with it is not dictated every day by the ebb and flow of the business or by the whims of the marketplace. They worked hard to lift themselves above the daily fray. They were able to do so because they were (and still are) driven by their passions to be their best and achieve their goals.

Consider a different example. Think about certain sports stars in the limelight, those whose energy and dedication to excellence are so intense that it fairly oozes from their pores. The one that pops into my head is Dustin Pedroia, the Boston Red Sox's All-Star second baseman. Pedroia is so plugged into the game, so excited to play baseball, it seems as though he would play for no salary.

Sidelined for much of the 2010 season with a broken foot, he nevertheless was in the dugout for every game, on crutches. Red Sox fans could sense his frustration at being sidelined, yet we could also see on his face the same eagerness and engagement that he has when he's on the field. He was champing at the bit to be back playing the game he loves and excels at, the game for which he won Rookie of the Year and Most Valuable Player awards in consecutive years (2007 and 2008, respectively).

What goes into that attitude? What shapes that approach to our chosen fields? What makes people like Dustin Pedroia and my friend Tim excel while another guy in the same field just plugs along, not deriving a lot of joy from his workaday life? The core driver may seem beyond words. But I think it's essentially a positive attitude toward life, an innate optimism, and a passion at one's core that makes it unthinkable to do anything halfway.

Ian Bostridge, the English tenor, opera star, and lieder singer, perhaps said it best when explaining to an interviewer how he approaches his art. "You can't stand there singing prettily. You have to seize the audience and not let go until you leave the stage. You have to burn. If you don't, it's a waste of time. Why bother?"

Exactly.

What kind of people do you want to associate with? What kind of people do you want to work for, to have on your team? Don't you want a guy like Dustin Pedroia, Ian Bostridge or my friend Tim? Absolutely.

You do because you connect to and want to share in their passion, enthusiasm, and optimism. And frankly, that enthusiasm, that passion for doing what they love and their optimism are contagious. Imagine being part of a team led by a guy like one of them, aiming for perfection in everything they do.

They endeavor not for perfection for its own sake, but rather because they know they're always capable of doing something better, with perfection as the ultimate aim. They go all out for that new level of excellence the next time they try. So even when they fall short in their own eyes, we know the result is going to be pretty damn good.

Does Pedroia bat 1.000? No. Does he ever make an error in the infield? Sure he does. Does Bostridge ever miss a note or fail to satisfy himself with a given performance? Of course. But the energy each expends in striving for his own version of excellence is, for them, a reward in itself.

It's also a beacon for their future journeys toward perfection, a baseline on which to build their next quest for success. Fueling that effort, always, is their optimism, their enthusiasm, and their passion for doing what they love. And I say, God bless them. The world needs more people like them.

155

Cut Through Employees' Workday Realities

After college, I was thrilled to land a job as a newspaper reporter, even though the pay was paltry. In the years after the *Washington Post*'s Bob Woodward and Carl Bernstein broke the Watergate story, being a reporter seemed like the sexiest, most exciting job for a recent college graduate.

While it certainly had its bracing moments, on balance it was a pretty tedious and boring job day-in and day-out. As a suburban beat reporter, I found myself sitting in interminable evening meetings of town finance committees, sewer commissions, school boards, and the like, filing my stories, ever alert for a breaking *Big Story*. Aside from a couple of local crime stories, none came my way, which is kind of the way it is in that business.

While they certainly worked hard throughout the process of uncovering the Watergate mess, and deserved the plaudits they received as a result, Woodward and Bernstein essentially got lucky to have their *Big Story* fall into their laps on a slow news night, a Saturday night, by the way, when they were taking their turn on the weekend night desk.

Sure, I got the chance to quench my desire to do lots of creative writing in fulfilling the obligation to write feature articles about local personalities and events.

Yet I soon reached the conclusion that about ninety percent of my workday was spent on mundane tasks and, at best, about ten percent involved truly interesting work, stuff that challenged me and helped me justify showing up for work every day. Over the years, I've reached a parallel conclusion about most work. Unless you're among the small minority of people who are doing what you truly love, it's likely that that 90/10 split holds true.

Ninety percent of your workday consists of tending to tedious tasks and dealing with hassles that you'd rather not have to. The remaining ten percent of your day involves doing what you like to do, being challenged, using the skills for which you have trained.

Okay, maybe you'll quibble about the 90/10 split. Maybe you'll say it's 75/25, 60/40 or 50/50. But I don't think you'd disagree that much of the work that people do is banal, tedious, and often a series of hassles getting in the way of letting them do what they excel at. I don't want to be overly negative here because I know that there are plenty of people who enjoy their work, including the dull parts.

But my point is that I believe this is a truism of work life and that managers and leaders must always bear it in mind. While it's tempting for a manager or leader to assume that everyone shares his/her enthusiasm for the organization and its vision, the truth is likely less than that.

The reality is that most people toiling on factory floors or in cubicles show up every day for the paycheck and benefits, trying to perform their jobs well and to their bosses' satisfaction, hoping that they get the promotions and raises they feel they've earned or, in times of economic downturns, hoping they don't get laid off.

When communicating in such an environment, then, it's critical to cut through the cynicism and ennui that inevitably exist in many corners of the organization, bred by the reality of people doing things they'd rather not be doing.

In a panel discussion I once participated in on the topic of communicating with employees, one fellow opined that leaders and managers must always strive to be "plain spoken" and honest in their communications, avoiding artificiality and obfuscation. I seconded that notion, but added the following corollary. "Yes, that's right," I said. "Be honest and plainspoken. But equally important is making sure your communications are relevant to the target audience."

Specifically, I said, make it pertinent to peoples' location (in a multi-site company), their specific area of responsibility or function, and their job title, etc. It's not helpful to communicate a carbon copy message to all audiences without accommodating the differences inherent in their position, responsibilities and physical location.

Relevance often is as easy as answering the top questions on employees' minds, particularly during stressful times: "What does this mean to me?" and "What am I supposed to do with this information?" The answers to those questions obviously vary on the basis of the assorted factors of the specific job assignment. It's the manager's job to answer those questions in a way relevant to his/her own particular unit, team or operation.

Accommodating those differences in our communications can bring meaning to people, helping them connect the dots and find the link between what they do and the larger purpose of the organization.

To that end, communications should be driven by centralized content (i.e., the big message) and localized relevance (i.e., linking the larger message to the everyday local realities that people deal with). We won't erase the mundane banalities of people's workaday realities, but we may open their eyes to the larger context so that they can see "the big picture" better and gain an enhanced appreciation of purpose, even in the midst of the daily workplace tedium and hassles.

Stay Open to New Technologies

It has been said that youth is overrated. That's probably because, in the eyes of their elders, younger people seem always to attach themselves to the latest technology as though they had discovered the ultimate, and all previous iterations become instant antiques.

While there may be some truth to that youthful view, think back to a particular technology that, at the time, was written about in every news medium, and talked about everywhere. Where is that technology today and how is it affecting our ability to communicate and do our jobs better?

Apple's Newton, while innovative for its time, was ultimately a failure. Yet it hinted at an important cultural shift and technological breakthrough. Future approaches, in the form of PDAs like the Palm Pilot and, later, smartphones like the iPhone, fixed its shortcomings and realized the full benefits that Newton's developers had hoped for, even if they hadn't fully understood where their idea would go.

Reminiscing recently with a friend I used to work with, I recalled a shared experience that still gives me pause about our attitudes regarding modern communications tools and the judgment of our elders.

A number of years ago, I was an account supervisor for a small public relations agency in New York. Mind you, this was 1986 when office computers were not yet common in the office. Sure, they were making in-roads, particularly in larger organizations. The IBM PC was well on its way to displacing the established Wang word processors. A hugely successful company of the same name made the "Wang" the first common office automation system.

Wang would soon cease to exist because it failed to take PCs seriously and adapt accordingly. At the time, my firm used a mix of IBM Selectric and Smith Corona portable electric typewriters. (Yes, I know. I'm dating myself here, straight out of *Mad Men*.)

Two co-workers and I thought it was time to bring computers into our operation. The three (considerably older) partners who owned the firm were skeptical. But they agreed to let us do our homework and develop a comprehensive cost-benefit analysis, which we did after much legwork and number crunching.

The day we presented our findings, the three partners gathered in the agency conference room, each bearing dubious looks, as we walked them through our findings and recommendations, detailing the efficiency improvements computers would allow us.

After thanking us for our after-hours work and acknowledging the persuasiveness of our arguments and thoroughness of our research, they decided against modernizing. It wasn't for lack of funds. It was their deep-seated skepticism of new technology. I will never forget the dismissive response of the senior partner as he paused from puffing on his pipe. (That's back when people smoked in offices.)

"Will these computers help the account executives write any better? I doubt it."

Frankly, this was completely beside the point. But never mind. The discussion was over.

About a year later, I left that firm for another in Boston (which, by the way, used Honeywell computers – again, I date myself). At the time of my departure, my former firm still hadn't computerized. In fact, the senior partner was still writing out everything in longhand on a legal pad, which his secretary (yes, we had secretaries back then) duly typed for him.

I remind myself of those long-ago words sometimes when I'm skeptical of a new technology, particularly one that might favorably impact communications and our ability to do business more efficiently. I'm wary of becoming like my old boss.

The first cell phone I ever used (rented for a trade show) was about the size of a shoe, though it was heavier. At the time, I didn't regard it as a business tool, even though it proved helpful at the trade show. It seemed more like an attention-getting novelty, which, as you will remember, most early cell phone users got a lot of – attention.

But as the cell phone shrunk in size and weight, as its cost came down and the quality of the connection improved, and as more people had them, the role of the cell phone as a business tool was set. Today, no one can imagine being without one. The list goes on – PDAs, laptops, smartphones, etc.

As you know, with each new technology, there is an adaptation curve, where the early adapters pay a premium price for an okay version with limited capabilities so that we late adapters can climb aboard when it's more ubiquitous, when mass production and marketplace competition have brought the price down.

Ubiquity also means the availability of more capabilities, more users with whom to share the common platforms, etc. So late adapters get more use from the devices because there are more people out there with whom we can communicate via ever more modes.

So let's come back to when they introduce the iPhone 4 that brought with it the "FaceTime" video-calling feature. While it was a nice feature and the advertising promoting it was compelling, before video calling on smartphones becomes a common means of communication, there would need to be a lot more capable devices on the market and in the hands of a lot more consumers. According to an October 12, 2010, report on Yahoo News:

> *"Jupiter Research on Tuesday said that Apple's latest generation iPhone will spur adoption of video calls but the trend is stymied because different devices don't talk to one another. Juniper predicted that . . . the percentage of smartphone users making video calls will remain below ten percent by the year 2015."*

As we contemplate new means of communications like video calling and other ways that improve our ability to connect with people around the clock around the world, are we better off for it? To rephrase the question my former boss asked, will these things make us better communicators?

(As it turned out, Jupiter's prognostication was pretty conservative. There are now sufficient numbers of iPhone users so that FaceTime indeed has become ubiquitous and useful – and likely far more than the ten percent they predicted.)

Tools like these are terrific and provide us a wider range of options to connect to more people in more places and times. They increase our availability to the people with whom we need or want to communicate.

But in the end, the importance of our willingness and ability to listen, to digest what we hear, and to respond appropriately doesn't change. That is the heart of effective communications, not the latest and greatest technology, whether it's an IBM Selectric, email, Twitter, Skype, a smartphone, or just an old-fashioned face-to-face meeting over a cup of coffee.

Set Boundaries Between Business and Personal

In the "good old days," bringing your work home was pretty rare. Usually, it meant after-dinner perusal of a few pieces of inter-office mail that we hadn't gotten around to that day. Perhaps it meant a client dinner that included one's spouse or a Saturday morning round of golf with the boss or client or both.

Today, bringing your work home is standard operating procedure, in light of leaner workforces, spawned by multiple layoffs that pile additional tasks on everyone. But our extended work hours are also being fueled by the proliferation of smartphones and the Internet, which enable round-the-clock communications with everyone in the company, no matter where in the world they may be at any given moment of the day, or day of the week.

In fact, we'd better have a good reason for failing to respond to an important weekend email. Vacations used to be sacrosanct and would serve as a valid reason for being out of touch, as did being on an airplane at 35,000 feet. Today, it seems, the only airtight excuse is being unconscious in a hospital's intensive care unit.

It's amusing to see people on vacation staring into a smartphones, tapping out messages while lounging in the sun on a sandy beach. We've all heard the anecdotes of how iPhones have intruded on deeply personal situations, like weddings and funerals. We know of spouses who "lay down the law" about "no emails" while on vacation. (Wink wink, nudge nudge. "But only if he/she catches me.") I had to laugh at a former client who called me on his cell phone while on a Caribbean cruise with his family, because he could.

> Me: *"I can't hear you. Why are you whispering?"*
> Boss: *"So my wife won't hear me. I'm not supposed to be calling the office."*
> Me: [LOL]

Modern technology's advance runs on parallel tracks with our expectations as to what it can and should do for us. The archetypal story, perhaps apocryphal, concerns the young businessman who happily discovers he can send and receive email while flying to his destination. He's thrilled and immediately is tapping away on his laptop. Suddenly, he loses the connection. He's outraged, as though this new capability has always been an entitlement.

This ratcheting up of expectations also manifests itself when, during teleconferences, people apologize, as though they've done something wrong, because their Internet connection was down and they weren't able to access the materials distributed beforehand.

The ability to send and receive email at all times and most locations also means that underlings strive to impress the boss (and one-up one another) by staying in touch during vacations or family emergencies or emailing the boss in the wee hours of the morning, privately gloating over a 2:00 AM time stamp.

This is getting out of hand. Technology has made it too easy for our work lives to intrude on our personal lives. So managers, especially senior managers, need to set boundaries between their employees' personal lives and the business.

The increased access technology provides us does not excuse rude intrusions, nor does it lessen the critical and central importance of healthy personal lives, particularly if those lives involve other people like spouses, children, and parents. As my friend pointed out in an email discussion on this topic, yes, people need to be "fluent in new technologies," but managers must "still respect their employees' personal space."

Managers must be proactive and explicit in setting those boundaries. That means prohibiting email contacts during vacations and family time, except when dire circumstances otherwise loom. Each business is different and, of course, that boundary will necessarily be vague and vary from one organization to another.

I was somewhat pleased at the news a friend told me about his company, a "new technology" dot-com firm. He witnessed a colleague getting scolded by their boss for sending everyone a business-related email over the weekend. Wow.

The blurring of the line between our personal and business lives has a potentially adverse impact on the quality of our work. We can't be effective in our jobs unless we are whole, unique persons, and we can't be whole without that clear distinction.

What a "Sense of Urgency" Means

Through good times and bad, through crises and times of change, businesses that thrive, grow, and succeed are those best able to maintain a sense of urgency.

But what does it mean to maintain a "sense of urgency?"

Many people equate urgency to lots of tasks being done quickly and frantically. Unfortunately, too many people buy into that myth. And that's exactly the wrong approach when a business is contending with a crisis or profound changes. While complacency is certainly the wrong way to respond to challenging circumstances, a false sense of urgency can often be more damaging.

In his book, "A Sense of Urgency," John P. Kotter ably explains the difference between the three responses and provides a useful guide for businesspeople facing change, crises, and challenges. Kotter, the Konosuke Matsushita Professor of Leadership Emeritus at Harvard Business School, has been lecturing and writing about leadership for years.

He has authored several outstanding books on the subject in the past decade that have become invaluable for today's business leaders, most notably: "Leading Change," "The Heart of Change" and "Our Iceberg is Melting." "A Sense of Urgency" carries forward and develops the themes of the previous three while folding in and updating much of what he learned in the intervening years.

The essence of true urgency lies in *"doing the right things the right way."* It is "ridding one's self of unproductive tasks that add little value to the organization, but tend to clog managers' calendars and impede necessary action." It's not allowing subordinates to "delegate tasks up" to you. It's that, and much more.

No doubt you've dealt with managers who want to appear to be operating with urgency. They run from meeting to meeting (often arriving late), over-scheduling their days, always checking their smartphone, coming into the office early and leaving late. Perhaps you've even been guilty of this kind of false urgency. According to Kotter (and based on my own observations), managers like this tend not to get a lot accomplished and rarely contribute to solving the immediate crises. Kotter says that this kind of behavior, operating with a false sense of urgency, is aimless, "frenetic behavior leading to exhaustion and stress."

Kotter defines complacent behavior as "unchanging activity that ignores the organization's opportunities or hazards, focusing inward." While complacency is built on a feeling that the status quo is basically fine, false urgency is built on a platform of anxiety and anger. By contrast, the true sense of urgency is action that is alert, fast moving, and focused externally on important issues.

That external focus is so important that Kotter devotes an entire chapter to it. In fact, bringing the outside world in is one of his four tactics to achieve true urgency.

As noted, a complacent organization is one that is inwardly focused. He writes, "An inwardly focused organization inevitably misses new opportunities and hazards coming from competitors, customers, or changes in the regulatory environment. When you don't see opportunities or hazards, your sense of urgency drops."

It's like being in a sealed room. You're breathing the same air repeatedly. No wonder it becomes stale. Bringing in fresh air from the outside world can take many forms, and Kotter cites a number of examples. For instance, bringing in the voice of the customers helps the organization become more cognizant of what it's doing right (and wrong) and how it might improve its products, services, and customer support in ways that assure and improve customer loyalty. (See *"Listen to the Customer's Voice,"* page 72.)

The outside world, as Kotter notes, is a constantly changing beast, with new challenges always popping up. New technologies arise that could mean the death knell of your business or, conversely, make your business more valuable if you leverage those technologies effectively.

An important component of urgency, which Kotter only obliquely mentions in this book, is the central role played by communications. Unfortunately, he falls into the usual trap of referring to organizational communications repeatedly in terms of tactics, in the context of a corporate function performing various tasks. In fact, strategic internal communications are implicit in and a requisite of truly urgent behavior, helping assure that the outside world is brought in – though he fails to say so.

If Kotter ever writes an updated version, I hope that he would add a chapter about communications. In it, he should explain that leaders and managers operating with urgency must be clear in their communications and keep their people in the loop. They must engage regularly in lively discussion, dialogue, and debate inside the company, and assure that the information they impart to the organization is both timely and relevant.

Despite Kotter's oversight and his omission of that key point, it's a fine book with some important counsel for today's manager.

Keep Employee Recognition Simple

Recognition is among the purest, most effective ways of communicating with employees. Recognizing people is also one of the best ways to reinforce the behaviors that support a business' purpose, vision and strategy.

Why, then, do so many companies and managers do such a poor job of it? A lot of bosses don't even say "thank you" when an employee puts in extra effort, as though to say, "So what? It's his job, isn't it?"

I once participated in an intriguing online discussion on Linked In at its Employee Communication and Engagement section that lasted for several weeks. There were a lot of predictable answers to the question about how best to recognize and reward employees, involving both narrowly focused and complicated methods, as well as tired, conventional actions.

I'm pleased to note, however, that the recurring theme of the discussion was that the simple "thank you" and acknowledgment go far, especially when received from the CEO and other senior executives. Recognition needn't always involve tangible rewards or money, nor must it be overly complicated.

Here's an entry in the discussion I liked. "[Saying] 'thank you' for a job well done goes a long way . . . I hear stories in focus groups about how good people felt when a boss, manager, [or the] CEO popped by and said thanks; how [it made their day when] the senior manager took a few minutes to say 'hello' (and perhaps 'thank

you'); [or, conversely] how bad and deflated others [felt] when they poured their energies into something, only to feel ignored and inconsequential; how senior managers visiting a site/department whisked in and out without a word to employees, [making] them feel like they didn't count." (See *"The Value of Saying 'Thank You',"* page 20.)

Toward improving the internal climate, one person cut to the core meaning of thanking people, noting, "Simple courtesy and respect. Two simple things that most of us were taught at an early age, and if we were not fortunate enough to have received this in our youth, at least most know how good it makes you feel to be treated with courtesy and respect."

At base, it's the CEO and his/her senior staff that determine the strategy and direction of the organization. So when individual contributors and/or teams are doing the good work that drives the organization toward those ends, the top people would be wise to set the standard and acknowledge it by saying "thanks."

A number of discussion participants wrote about using internal communications vehicles to spotlight people's good work. One typical comment was, "If you have a corporate newsletter or an Intranet site filled with articles about what's happening in your organization, well-written, compelling stories that highlight individual achievement can be your cheapest and most effective way to recognize deserving employees and teams." That's fine, provided the primary (and first) acknowledgment comes directly from the person's manager or a more senior person in the organization.

The following story, posted in the online discussion, was so poignant that I include it here. It speaks for itself.

"Some years back, a custodial employee working for one of my clients came up with an ingenious way to eliminate a slip hazard for

customers on wet or snowy days. A story about it, with a photo of the employee, was featured in the company newsletter. This company routinely mailed copies of its newsletter to the children of any employees highlighted within its pages, with a personalized note that read, 'Your daddy's picture appears on page 2.' Several weeks later, management held a staff meeting and invited questions about their quality improvement program. The custodian rose to his feet and reported that the day his two children received the newsletter, he'd been greeted with a hero's welcome when he got home. His youngsters wanted to hear how his picture came to be in 'the paper.' The kids had subsequently brought the newsletter to school for show-and-tell, and the teacher posted it on the school bulletin board for a week. His kids felt like celebrities at school, he said, as if their dad had been on the cover of Time *magazine. He went on to acknowledge that he'd always assumed they were somewhat ashamed of the janitorial work their father did for a living. This expression of pride from his own children, he said, was the most personally rewarding experience in his entire thirty-year career with the company, and if this was the kind of thing management meant by 'quality improvement,' he wanted them to know he was ready to do anything he could to help. With that, he sat back down . . ."*

How Office Small Talk Improves Our Work

It's called "water-cooler talk," or just shootin' the breeze. It's the often non-productive chitchat that occurs in every office every day of the week, especially Monday. And it's the bane of many productivity-obsessed bosses. But is it communications? Is there any value in it? Should it be discouraged?

Like anything, too much of something is probably, well, too much. Nothing of value happens in a business environment if people spend the bulk of their time talking about topics unrelated to the business at hand – the NFL playoffs, the recent episode of their favorite TV serial drama, stock tips, a big family event, complaints about the weather, golf scores, personal health issues, children, grandchildren, vacation plans, and the like.

But this kind of internal communication, if practiced in moderation, is indeed valuable.

Let's face it: people comprise businesses. And these people have lives away from the job – families, celebrations, illnesses and personal tragedies, hobbies, pet peeves, and passions unrelated to their 9-to-5 responsibilities.

Knowing a person's interests outside the office or factory floor often gives us clues about what makes them tick, how they operate, how they think, who they are, what they're truly good at. Having such insights into and connections with the people we work with regularly, or even occasionally, can be valuable in the long run.

For instance, common interests can create foundations for

establishing and sustaining important working relationships. It's the proverbial icebreaker that gives us entry to tackling difficult and challenging work-related subjects day-in and day-out.

The ability to open a Monday morning business meeting with a brief rehash of a Sunday afternoon NFL game eases us into a discussion of how to address a vexing customer relations issue or a challenging technical glitch. Or it enables a manager to soften the blow of some bad news. Maybe it serves as an appropriate metaphor for or as a segue to the topic at hand.

Small talk can also help us connect with people at remote locations. It can be fun working with people in other locations when your respective favorite professional or college football, baseball, hockey, or basketball teams play each other. You can speculate ahead of the big game, needle one another, and gloat a little if your team wins or make lame excuses if your team loses. It's all in good fun.

We've all had to work with people about whom we know nothing; people who think the personal side of our lives is an inappropriate topic for office discussions; people who dive straight into the topic at hand every time, with no preamble discussion beyond a perfunctory "good morning." Think about your working relationships with those kinds of people. Would the word "sterile" describe it? Did you feel you could trust them? Did you enjoy working with them?

Consider the opposite. Suppose you work for or with someone who opens conversations by asking how your son is doing in his first year away at college, or about your wife's job with a company that isn't doing well, or inquiring about the health of your ailing mother. You're going to have a different kind of relationship with that type of boss than the former.

This person operates on an entirely different plane. Instead of opening the meeting with a terse "let's get down to business," by spending a few moments to acknowledge the private issues that may be distracting you at the moment, your colleague indicates a personal interest in your life and an awareness that you may not be on top of your game that day. Showing that we are concerned about each other's welfare and personal challenges is a sign of respect for her/him as a whole person.

There's still another side to office chitchat, with a business benefit, perhaps. Suppose a water cooler discussion one day reveals the fact that a co-worker lives next door to someone you know as a valuable contact in your particular field. Maybe your water cooler friend is in IT and you're in sales. As a tech guy, maybe he didn't think of his neighbor as a potential customer. But you know the name and so you ask your office buddy for an introduction, or perhaps you finagle an invitation to the Christmas party he and his wife are hosting, where you hope to meet this neighbor. There's nothing wrong with that, especially if it leads to new business.

Similarly, maybe someone's outside hobby has some bearing on the business that they hadn't thought of. Or maybe it's the realization that a new hire's single-digit golf handicap indicates the kind of dedication and perseverance you're looking for as a new member to your team.

We are all people for whom the workaday routine is but one aspect of our lives. To recognize that is good. It's a sign of respect for our colleagues as individuals, acknowledging their unique selves that they bring to the job every day.

Find Your Valuable Contributors

Lessons that are meaningful and useful in our work can come from anywhere, sometimes even our own youth. I learned an important one about the value of a strong work ethic during my college years.

My summers at that time were filled with labor-intensive jobs. Often, it entailed working alongside other young men that, without the opportunity of college or the inclination to go, would likely do pretty much the same kind of work for the rest of their lives.

During two summers, I worked for what was then known as the "California Division of Forestry" (CDF), fighting fires in the Sierra foothills in Calaveras County. Among the local men I worked with, there was an initial arms' length attitude toward me and two other coworkers who, come Labor Day, would leave for college, a world they knew nothing of.

Sometimes, they didn't use our names, addressing us simply as: "Hey! College Boy!"

It was not a term of endearment. Nevertheless, we came to respect one another over time through our shared experience of working and fighting wild fires.

In many ways, those hard-working fellows were way ahead of us. Coming from local blue collar families, they understood from an early age the importance of hard work and the central role it played in one's life, helping them attain independence and the ability to support a family. I was just a self-involved College Boy, with no real responsibilities at the time.

Ken McCrank (his real name) was typical. Married and already a father, Ken was just a couple years older than I. He had previously worked at the only major employer in the area, a cement mine and refinery. Ken was relieved to put that dreadfully dirty and hazardous job behind him, happy to call himself an employee of the State of California, with all its job security and benefits.

I came to respect him for his solid work ethic and, in hindsight, for the life lessons his attitude gave me.

At the CDF, when not fighting fires, which could be dirty, exhausting and sometimes-dangerous work, we were nevertheless working hard. We did what the captain told us to do: paint buildings, continually (or so it seemed) wash and wax fire trucks, or cut firebreaks in anticipation of potential wild fires.

On a cloudless 105-degree day, Ken and I were assigned to dig a ditch for a new water line. Not eager to labor in the hot sun, I set about scheming to get out of the task, inventing weak excuses to postpone the inevitable. After a bit, Ken laughed at me. "If you'd spend as much time working as you do trying to figure out how not to work, you'd get a lot more done and be finished a lot sooner," he said, as he grabbed the pick and started digging the ditch. There was no arguing his point. I deserved the good-natured ribbing.

Ken and others like him with whom I worked those many summers ago gave me a deeper understanding of and appreciation for the work ethic that they brought to the job.

In my work today, helping companies communicate effectively with their employees, including hourly workers who are often a lot like Ken, memories of those college summers sometimes come back to me. Ken's sweaty, grinning face is etched in my memory as I consider how best to engage the front line workers in the company's larger mission.

176

Too often, managers view their workers in the abstract and not as fellow human beings also striving to contribute value to a cause greater than their own. I've seen situations where such employees sense managers' aloofness and respond appropriately by disconnecting. The job becomes just a paycheck. There is no emotional connection and no investment on their part.

That's a lost opportunity for the company, because the value of people who are proud of their work and their employer, engaged in the business, and desiring a mutual commitment from their managers is priceless.

It pained me when I once heard a factory worker say, "I check my brain at the door every day" because no one cared what he thought, what he had learned on the job during his many years there, or how he might contribute to improving the operation. What he was saying was that he was not committed to the organization because the message he got was that his company was not committed to him, and that it didn't seek his commitment to the job.

That likely was not the intent. But it was probably the result of a manager who didn't listen, who didn't solicit employees' ideas and input, who failed to connect with his people. In turn, he failed to recognize the inherent value that the front line workers bring to the operation.

Ken McCrank taught me a long time ago that everyone in the organization can and should be a valuable contributor. And shame on the manager who fails in his/her responsibility to connect with them, to engage them in the business, and to build commitment to a common purpose.

A New Way of Seeing Things

"One's destination is never a place,
but a new way of seeing things."

Henry Miller
Novelist
1891-1980

Examine Your Point-of-View

If you've ever lived in or near, or spent time in a coastal community, you know the odors that emanate from the estuaries and tidal marshes, especially at low tide. Familiar though not altogether pleasant, the distinctive odors are emitted by the various creatures and microscopic life forms that inhabit such places through their life stages: living, dying, dead and decaying.

We typically associate that agglomeration of odors with all things related to being at the seaside. We think of it as "the smell of the sea." But that's just because of our point of view.

To a sea-going fisherman or sailor, someone who spends most of his days on the ocean, that same odor is "the smell of land." As he sets sail and heads out to sea, that odor fades away and the dominant sense is the clean salt air. In the reverse, as we head inland away from the seashore, the odors die away and the aromas of plants, flowers and life on land predominate.

At the point where the scents of the shoreline prevail, landlubbers and men of the sea share a common sensual experience. It's the same odors, smelling the same to both, yet identified with contradictory terminology.

It's all a matter of perspective and what one is most familiar with.

The same is true with life, including life within a business organization. People come to various challenges and opportunities with a set of biases that spring, quite naturally, from the environment in which they operate every day and the experiences they have there. A typical company's various functions present a case in point.

Gather managers from different operations in a room to deal with a particular challenge and you're likely to get perceptions that reflect their areas of expertise and focus.

The finance guy sees the challenge through a fiscal lens. The sales manager comes at it with the bias of the customer. The human resources manager sees the internal people implications. The supply chain manager infers the impact on logistics, parts inventory and pricing. And so on.

In the same way, people at different levels of the organization or geographic locations have similarly divergent perceptions of challenges and opportunities. It's not at all unusual for people based in the headquarters offices to see things considerably different from people in the field, at remote locations, facilities or factories.

Being on the ground dealing directly with customers is an entirely different experience than inhabiting the upper floors of the company's head offices. On the one hand, the person is confronting the real world impact of the company's products and policies, while the other is operating largely within a theoretical construct. At the same time, however, the person at the headquarters office may see the larger nuances of challenges and opportunities that the front line guy misses because he's too close to it.

Both smell the same odors, yet it's land to one and sea to the other.

Both perceptions are right and both imply realities and insights that, together, add value to the corporation's pursuit of its mission. Problems arise when that distinction is not understood by one another, not taken into account and not fully appreciated. Breaking down the walls of perception to see through another's eyes is key to the organization's ability to fulfill its mission, to achieve collective superiority, as it should.

Instead of a pointless argument over what amounts to a semantic difference, it's better to know and appreciate that your landlubber friend smells the same thing as you, even though he expresses it differently. It's the first step in the process toward achieving collective excellence.

Expand Your Self-Perception

How we think and talk about our business truly defines what we are. If, for instance, you see your business as simply that of a widget manufacturer, then it's likely that's how you present your company and, by extension, how your customers perceive you. That may seem obvious, but that kind of perception can also hem you in and limit your opportunities. And it might mean that you miss opportunities that you are capable of tackling.

Step back and think of what it is that you're truly selling your customers. You say you manufacture widgets and sell them to a discrete target audience. In fact, you are helping your customers use your widgets to solve their unique challenges.

Maybe your most valuable skills lie in your understanding of a customer's challenge and how one particular widget you make (instead of a competitor's) might solve that for them. So that makes you a solutions-based company.

The value you bring your customers goes beyond merely filling orders with the widgets you make; it's making their lives simpler and saving them money by solving their problems. Allow customers to see you in that light, rather than simply as a maker of the products they buy from you, and a new world of opportunity will open up.

This is not a new idea. It's what countless companies have done, most notably, IBM, which, back in the mid-1990s, shifted its focus from that of a maker and marketer of computer hardware to a service-oriented consulting firm. It's also where General Electric has gone with many of its businesses, delivering more value to its customers and more profit to its balance sheet.

It all starts with your own self-perception.

Think about Ford Motor Company for a moment. One of America's oldest companies, Ford makes cars and trucks, right? Sure, their factories crank out products that enable us to haul people and goods from Point A to Point B. But the people at Ford developed a new understanding of and appreciation for what they do and what they are.

Back in the mid-2000s, they started thinking of themselves as akin to a software company, according to then-executive vice president and president for Americas (now CEO), Mark Fields.

Huh? What happened to the "motor heads" that shaped and defined Detroit the past one-hundred-plus years? What about the steel and rubber that built that industry?

In the kind of insightful article for which the magazine is known, *Fast Company* (April 2010, by Paul Hochman) revealed a new Ford being created around the notion of keeping drivers in touch via twenty-first century technology: Bluetooth, smartphones, laptop computers, MP3 players, GPS, etc.

Ford did it with its own "Sync" on-board Bluetooth platform built on Microsoft's Windows CE operating system. It allows a driver, without taking his/her hands off the steering wheel, to use voice commands to make phone calls, select radio stations, or choose music (by genre, artist, or song title).

And that's just the beginning. Soon, Ford owners will be able to navigate to their destination, locate a nearby McDonald's restaurant or Exxon service station, get a local weather forecast, and more, all with voice commands as they speed down the Interstate, with both hands on the steering wheel and eyes on the road. Your Ford's Sync system is designed to learn your voice, your unique phrasing, your musical tastes, and begin to anticipate your commands.

Initially, Ford was hoping merely to create an on-board communications system that would compete with GM's hugely successful OnStar phone, concierge, and roadside assistance system. In fact, they've leapfrogged their cross-town rivals. But it didn't happen until they thought of themselves as more than a carmaker offering a me-too product. And then their thinking expanded beyond the confines of a typical passenger car.

Unlike GM's static OnStar system, Ford's Sync platform is designed to evolve symbiotically with the handheld devices owners carry with them in their Ford vehicles, as well as how their use of those devices evolves.

As the *Fast Company* article notes, this is a huge marketing advantage for Ford: "The great thing for Ford, of course, is that the more Ford improves a customer's favorite handheld device, the more likely it is that people will want to carry their handheld devices into a Ford."

Ford's then-CEO Alan Mulally cleverly linked these new doings with the founder's vision. "We're committed to this thing," he said. "Look, this is part of Henry's [Ford] vision. 'Opening the highways to all mankind.' I think this is the way to do it."

It boggles the imagination to think that a car company could expand its thinking from between the shoulders of a paved road to the limitless frontiers of computer software and the Internet.

Frankly, in these times of profound change, companies that don't likewise rethink what they are and what they do will soon be left in the dust as their competitors evolve with the changing world and speed ahead into the future.

Think what's possible if you also rethink what you do that way.

Connect to Your Modern Day Pen Pals

As a member of Miss Beyers' sixth grade class at Proctor Terrace Elementary School in Santa Rosa, CA, I was part of a project in which she engaged the class to connect us all with pen pals, kids our own age from around the world.

My pen pal was a girl from Adelaide, Australia. I've forgotten her name but remember the upshot of our correspondence:

- Comparing and contrasting our schoolwork;

- What we were studying;

- How we spent our free time;

- Our favorite musical groups (her, Beatles; me, Beachboys);

- What it was like living in Adelaide and Santa Rosa; and

- What we aspired to do and be, etc.

We exchanged photos of one another and wrote about our pets and friends. That she was in the middle of summer while I was in winter, and vice-versa, intrigued us both.

I eagerly looked forward to her letters and enjoyed the hand-written correspondence, as long it lasted, about a year, tailing off once we had exhausted our troves of cultural idiosyncrasies from our respective countries.

This recollection came back to me when I found myself engaged in a Linked In online discussion about the relative differences between internal and external communications. In such instances, I "converse" with strangers around the world, like modern day pen pals.

In this particular discussion, I responded to a point made by a gentleman from Mumbai, India, about a topic started by a woman in Moscow, who works for a company headquartered in Norwich, UK. Others involved in the discussion included people from Ottawa, London, Rochester (UK), and Minneapolis. And all this was being done in real time.

If I could travel back in time to tell her about all this, what would Miss Beyers think? It isn't like my pen pal days when letters could take one to two weeks to traverse the Pacific Ocean. These are instantaneous communications. (Do kids even have "pen pals" anymore? I guess that's what Facebook is for.)

How far we've come. We are now able to track down and reconnect with former high school and college classmates with whom we've been out of touch for years, an activity that would have been virtually impossible a mere fifteen years ago, then engage in on-going email correspondence, renewing old friendships

Genealogical research that used to require extensive travel to dig through dusty records in distant repositories can now be done online, enabling us to find old photos and artifacts, and connect quickly to distant cousins, known and previously unknown, no matter where in the world they may be, to share memories and knowledge of one's grandparents and distant relatives.

Meanwhile, my college-age son made lasting friendships via online, real-time video games with people from around the world: France, Germany, Israel, Japan, and Russia, as well as Massachusetts and the U.S. No doubt he has learned far more about those people's personalities and interests than I did in the entire year of my pen pal correspondence.

It makes me wonder what's next. What further technological advancements can we expect in communications? And, more important, what will be their impact on our ability to expand our knowledge, to engage other people in topics of mutual interest? What will be their effect on improving cross-cultural understanding and how we perceive the wider world?

In making my point with the gentleman from Mumbai, I was able to look him up on Linked In and learn that he is head of corporate communications with a software company there. So I was able to make my comments more relevant than they might otherwise have been.

These new social media are profoundly affecting the way we do business today, too, both inside and outside our companies. The wiser companies are tapping into "the conversation" that is always occurring on the web about them. An October 26, 2010, article in *The Wall Street Journal* explained how Delta Air Lines eavesdrops on Twitter conversations when the topic is Delta.

The tracking effort proved quite beneficial. It enabled the company to short-circuit negative discussions and correct gross inaccuracies about them. At the same time, Delta developed greater loyalty and understanding among its customers, responding directly and promptly to address their real complaints about service problems in real time.

At its "Best Practices in Change and Employee Engagement Summit" in October 2010, co-sponsors Edelman Change & Employee Engagement, and Edelman Digital brought together a number of senior communications professionals in their New York City offices to discuss both the implications of social media like Twitter and Facebook on corporate communications, and their potential. In addition to the one hundred guests present in New York, some one thousand people participated via webcast.

One of the ten speakers, the former head of customer service for Comcast, explained how the company tapped into the web conversations about it, found a lot to be concerned about, and began addressing the negative commentary directly. Eventually, it was even able to put the web site "ComcastMustDie.com" out of business, deflating its reason for existence by merely responding proactively to contributors' actual complaints about Comcast's shoddy service.

Edelman created a special section on its web site to recap the Summit, complete with videos of all the presentations. Venues like Edelman's Summit and the subsequent Summit web pages magnify the limitless capabilities of the worldwide web.

This sort of collective connection is far more common now, some seven years later. Such conversations are occurring on a growing number of topics, and ever-greater synergies and spread of advanced ideas about social media continue in that manner as people leverage such events and web sites to share and spread new ideas and new thinking on a range of topics.

But you have to go look for it. You have to be hands-on in engaging all that the web has to offer. If you aren't already, you, too, can become part of that conversation, or any conversation, if you wish, no matter where you are: New York, Mumbai, Ottawa, London, Santa Rosa or Adelaide.

As with any such experiences, when we engage other people across national or cultural borders, we open ourselves to new ideas and new ways of seeing things, and make ourselves more complete and better people for it.

Carpe Diem

One sunny, summer Sunday morning, my wife and I were driving down a two-lane Maine country highway. It was a good, safe road, recently repaved, with broad shoulders and plenty of room for passing slower vehicles.

I was doing the speed limit of fifty-five miles per hour in a straight stretch when I saw a big semi tractor-trailer rig in the distance, coming toward us at about the same speed. As the truck neared, I could see it was a fully loaded flatbed trailer of assorted items. But I also noticed the load at the rear was not secured and appeared to be coming loose.

In the milliseconds as it got closer, as though in slow motion, I could see it was a vertically stacked pile of steel scaffolding parts at the back and, to my horror, it seemed about to fall off the truck right into our path. Our combined speed was probably more than one hundred miles per hour so there was little I could do in that split second. We passed one another in a flash, just as the metal tumbled sideways off the truck into my lane. In my rear view mirror, I could see it fall close behind us, near enough that we also heard the loud clattering of metal pipes on pavement.

And then the immensity of the moment hit me. The duration of a heartbeat made the difference between what had happened and what might have happened. The "might have" could well have meant our instantaneous deaths, or at least severe, life-threatening injuries, if the heavy metal scaffolding had landed on the hood of our car and crashed through the windshield, if I had braked instead of maintaining my speed. If, if, if. "What might have been" stayed with me for days, and still haunts me.

As a teenager and into my young adult years, I was often reckless and took a lot of unnecessary (sometimes stupid) risks, mostly involving outdoor sports like downhill skiing, back-country hiking, and mountain and rock climbing, sustaining my share of broken bones and other assorted scrapes, bruises and stitches. But never did I experience such a harrowing near-death experience as I did in that brief instant on the country highway.

In reality, it's the knowledge of what might have been that haunts me because, had I glanced away at that moment, I might never have known how close we had come to utter disaster.

Still, it gives me pause and a new insight into what has become the clichéd notion of fully appreciating the present, of being in the moment and making the most of it. Every day is a new day, with new opportunities, and every moment is fresh. Yet, we get lulled into our daily routines and time passes without our notice, or it passes too slowly in our eagerness for the next event.

We focus on the short term, the planned weekend activities, the coming vacation, and we forsake the moment we are in. Catch phrases like "Monday blues," "hump Wednesday" and "thank God it's Friday" become part of our regular office conversations, as though time can't move fast enough for us and there's always something better soon to come.

A rainy day may spoil our outdoor plans, but that doesn't mean it's an ugly day or that it's a lost day. We need to take them one at a time. I hate summer days that are hot and humid, or freezing wintry days because they limit my options and make me want to stay indoors. But it's still a distinctly separate day with its own identity, and I need to learn anew how to seize it and make the most of it.

The Latin phrase, "*Carpe diem,*" which means, "Seize the day," has become a cliché of sorts. I never studied Latin, so I had to go look up its origin, and learned that it was from a poem by the Roman poet, Horace. The poem translates into English as follows:

> *"Don't ask (it's forbidden to know) what end the gods will grant to me or you, Leuconoe. Don't play with Babylonian fortune-telling either.*
> *"It is better to endure whatever will be.*
> *"Whether Jupiter has allotted to you many more winters or this final one which even now wears out the Tyrrhenian sea on the rocks placed opposite — be wise, strain the wine, and scale back your long hopes to a short period.*
> *"While we speak, envious time will have {already} fled.*
> *"Seize the day, trusting as little as possible in the next."*

We need to learn to be present in the moment, to approach our everyday surroundings as though we're discovering them anew, as though we're tourists in our own hometowns.

We should greet each day as though it's our last, as though that scaffolding did in fact come crashing through our windshield. We should approach our own back yards as a frontier, and be with our friends as though we may never see them again. Let's vow to fully appreciate the moment, regardless of what we're doing: working or playing, laughing or crying.

See and Act Like An Outsider

Familiarity with our everyday reality can blind us to meaningful and critical nuances. It usually takes an outsider to sense, appreciate and bring to our attention what may be as obvious as the nose on our face. What got me thinking about this little truism is the "Green Monster," the famous leftfield wall in the Boston Red Sox's Fenway Park. Or, more precisely, how it once was shown to me.

The New England Sports Network (NESN) broadcasts virtually every Red Sox game, both at home and on the road. The exception is when ESPN or FOX Sports decide a particular game's import merits a national audience. While I prefer the commentary, sense of humor and insider observations of the regular NESN announcers, one ESPN broadcast opened my eyes to a wonderful little truth about the uniqueness of good old Fenway, the oldest ballpark in the Major League.

The most dominant feature of Fenway, as any Red Sox fan will tell you, is the "Green Monster," the thirty-seven-foot wall that shortens leftfield to 310 feet, Fenway's centerfield "triangle" being 420 feet. It creates a nightmare for visiting leftfielders, unsure how to play a careening line drive that may hit the wall at various angles ten, twenty or thirty feet above their heads.

Never before that particular ESPN broadcast did I fully appreciate the Green Monster, aside from its daunting height and knack for robbing long-ball hitters of likely home runs. During a lull in the action, ESPN focused one of its cameras closely on the wall and suddenly it became apparent, as the announcer noted, that there were dozens upon dozens of dings, dents, and pockmarks in the green sheet metal sheathing, testimony to the years of line drives and arching long balls that produced hits, many of which probably spelled the difference between victory and loss.

It gave me pause, and made me wonder which long-gone All Stars created which ding, dent and pockmark. Which ones came off Ted Williams' and Carl Yastrzemski's bats? Which did visiting batsmen, like Joe DiMaggio, Boog Powell, Harmon Killebrew, "Hammerin' Hank" Greenberg, Reggie Jackson, and others, create?

It conveyed a sense of history, like the still visible bullet holes in the exterior walls of the *École Militaire* that bear witness to the last firefight in Paris as it fell to the German *Wehrmacht* in June 1940.

It took an outsider to notice that little nuance, something that the local guys never mentioned. Sure, they were probably well aware of it. No doubt they can see the pockmarks in the sheathing every time they watch a line drive rebound fiercely off the wall.

But they don't see them. The dings are a fact of everyday life in Fenway and not worth a second thought, much less an NESN close-up or an exegesis about it. What does that tell us about how we conduct business, or go about our daily lives?

Coming home from an exotic foreign vacation, we try to hang on to the newness of everything as we return to the banalities of life back home. We promise ourselves that we'll look at every familiar facet of our life with new eyes and fresh insight. But we can't. It's not human nature to be able to bend reality and pretend that everything old is new again.

We need to learn to listen to that other opinion, that unique insight, even though it may seem off-the-wall. It's that other insight, that unique way of looking at things that can open new vistas to our everyday world, whether it be the world of commerce or that of our personal lives.

Our own Green Monsters have become something so familiar to us that they cease being monsters at all. They become a toy, like the bobble head "Wally" dolls sold at Fenway, the faux team mascot, a cute, smiling Sesame Street-like character that neutralizes the otherwise scary concept of a monster. It's a monster that is easy to live with, easy to conceive, easy to ignore in the wallpaper that surrounds our lives.

If we can bring in the outsider's view, or imbue ourselves with that view, we can see with new eyes the world with which we are so familiar.

We can be tourists in our own land and gain new insights into how we operate in that context, better able to be honest with ourselves about our weaknesses and strengths, about the dings in our own Green Monsters.

Playing the Concertina of Life

One day, I perused my bookshelves looking for something to read, a small paperback, preferably, because I was leaving on a trip the next day. My eye landed on an old book I hadn't read in years: "The Thousand Mile Summer," written in 1959 by Colin Fletcher.

Fletcher, a Welshman, fought with the Royal Marines in World War 2, then traveled the world before settling permanently in the United States in 1956.

He made his mark as the author of outdoor books and articles. His more noted titles were his second and third books, "The Man Who Walked Through Time," and "The Complete Walker," the former a memoir of his hike that covered the length of the Grand Canyon below the rim; the latter a comprehensive guidebook for aspiring back country hikers. "The Complete Walker," updated four times, became backpackers' Bible.

"The Thousand Mile Summer," his first book, was less well known. It concerns his hike up the spine of eastern California in 1958, from the Mexican border to Oregon, alongside the Colorado River, through the Mojave Desert, Death Valley, into the Sierra Nevada, and northward. It took exactly six months to the day, from March 8 to September 8. At the book's end, as he reflects on the experience and how he had told the tale, he writes the following:

"There is a difference in shape between a journey as it happens and a journey as you remember it. At the time, there it is—day after

roughly equal day. But when you look back afterward (and especially when you talk or write about it) memory pushes and pulls at time as if it were a concertina. The vivid moments expand, so that they stand out like cameos. The dull periods contract, until whole weeks become compressed into thin shims."

This paragraph stopped me in my tracks. If you think more broadly about "journey" to imply the many experiences that comprise our lives, it makes perfect sense. It's a splendid, fitting metaphor, the idea of life's memories as a concertina.

The daily routines, with all their ordinariness, are compressed into the thin shims, while those joyful moments, sometimes so brief and fleeting, expand, stand out and over-shadow everything else.

The clever and creative among us are able to weave the pleasurable moments into larger-than-life events. Sometimes, we exaggerate some details while ignoring others. Indeed, a good storyteller, one who is entertaining when relating personal experiences, is one who is able to play that concertina, expand the moments of joy and excitement to come alive and become something larger than they were.

Fletcher, who passed away in 2007 at the age of eighty-five, teaches us the importance of focus, of winnowing out that which is unimportant.

His tale examines in wonderful detail the unusual people he met along the trail, the beautiful vistas of the eastern Sierras he witnessed, the harsh heat of Death Valley, and all the rest. Yet the last several hundred miles toward the Oregon border, his tale speeds to a conclusion, thereby falling into the "thin shims" of his larger story. (He admits, "The last three weeks of the hike were dull.")

I think of his words a lot, assessing how I might approach each new day. Will it be a thin shim, or can I make it stand out like a cameo? In the end, it is we who make those choices for ourselves.

"Because it's there"

Knowing my love of adventure, a friend sent me a newspaper article about a twenty-nine-year-old family friend named Eli Andersen who had circumnavigated Graham Island standing atop and paddling a large surfboard. I'd never heard of Graham Island, but thanks to Google Maps, I found out, and I was even more impressed by the feat.

Graham comprises about half of the landmass of the Queen Charlotte Islands, BC, north of Vancouver Island, south of the Alaskan panhandle. It took Eli six weeks to paddle around Graham.

The notion of a wild adventure like that appeals to something deep in me and I was fascinated. I think that this young man touched on what it was when he said, "I like to lie down in my sleeping bag at night after I have made camp. I congratulate myself on a long paddle, or finding the ideal campsite, or had made good decisions. I pat myself on the back and say 'good job Eli, you did it.' I enjoy that feeling."

I know that feeling, too. It's an ineffable sense of accomplishment. It's reaching well beyond what you believe you are capable of doing and then doing it. It's deep fatigue, that feeling of tired, aching muscles telling you how difficult it was, and the comforting knowledge that you did it, a truth that no one can take away, proven by the fact of where you are at that moment.

It's crazy, isn't it, to engage in such dangerous ventures as paddling solo around an island in the northern Pacific Ocean. Why do we do it? As a college kid, much to my mother's horror, I hitchhiked and freight-hopped my way from Salem, OR, to the Grand Canyon, a distance of about 1,500 miles. And when I got there, I hiked to the bottom of the canyon.

Over the years, I've camped out under the stars in a remote corner of the Isle of Skye in Scotland; trained for and run six marathons; climbed Mt. Hood; nearly drowned while canoeing the St. Croix River in Maine overflowing its banks with the spring flood; climbed vertical rock walls; and hiked into the High Sierras numerous times. They were all tough, physically trying and sometimes-dangerous experiences, some more so than others. But, as we press to the edge of our own abilities and strengths, we gain confidence and a better understanding of our personal limits.

Why do I do it? In the case of the High Sierras, it's because when you can camp out at 11,000 feet, you get unbroken vistas of a hundred miles; a night sky full of trillions of bright stars; cold glacial melt water to drink; crisp, clean air to breathe; complete silence, save any wind; utter solitude; and the harsh beauty of sheer granite cliffs and high altitude, aquamarine lakes. You congratulate yourself in the knowledge of your accomplishment, how hard you worked to be able to see and experience it all, knowing that you are among the few people up to it.

Mountaineers always respond to the *"Why?"* question by saying, *"Because it's there."* Seems as good a reason as any. In fact, what that answer says is that they can imagine themselves atop a particular mountain, just as Eli could imagine himself circumnavigating Graham Island alone. To picture one's self doing something is tantamount to doing it. It's throwing down the gauntlet and daring one's self to do it. Failing is one thing, but failing to try is not acceptable.

That's the nub. *Not trying is unacceptable.*

Pres. Theodore Roosevelt, himself an avid and fearless adventurer, understood this truth. He once said:

> *"It is not the critic who counts; not the man who points out how the strong man stumbles, or where the doer of deeds could have done them better. The credit belongs to the man who is actually in the arena, whose face is marred by dust and sweat and blood, who strives valiantly; who errs and comes up short again and again; because there is not effort without error and shortcomings; but who does actually strive to do the deed; who knows the great enthusiasm, the great devotion, who spends himself in a worthy cause, who at the best knows in the end the triumph of high achievement and who at the worst, if he fails, at least he fails while daring greatly. So that his place shall never be with those cold and timid souls who know neither victory nor defeat."*

Another president, John F. Kennedy, challenged the nation to go to the moon, at the time a tremendously and unthinkably difficult test. "We choose to go to the moon in this decade," he said, "not because [it is] easy, but because [it is] hard, because that goal will serve to organize and measure the best of our energies and skills, because that challenge is one that we are willing to accept, one we are unwilling to postpone, and one which we intend to win. . ."

That statement, in a nutshell, defined for an era who we were as a nation, what our goals were; that we were fully aware of the risks of the mission, in the context of our confidence in our ability to do it. But to fail to try was not acceptable to the American spirit, and the nation as one eagerly rose to the president's challenge.

One's mountain needn't be a moon mission or an Alpine peak to conquer, or an island to paddle around. It can be something as close to home as a painting to conceive of and finish, a gourmet meal to plan, cook and serve, or a book to write and publish. And, it might be overcoming a job-related challenge.

Tales of adventures are merely internal human struggles writ large, and literally played out on a real life canvas. Edward Whymper, a late-nineteenth century English mountaineer and explorer, answered the "Why?" question with remarkable clarity:

> *"We who go mountain-scrambling have constantly set before us the superiority of fixed purposes or perseverance to brute force. . . [W]e know where there's a will there's a way; and we come back to our daily occupations better fitted to fight the battle of life, and to overcome the impediments which obstruct our paths, strengthened and cheered by the recollection of past labours, and by the memories of victories gained in other fields."*

In the overly formal language of the Victorian era, those words neatly sum up what I've long struggled to verbalize succinctly. After those exertions spent overcoming uniquely difficult obstacles, after stressing our bodies to the limit, after testing our will against the challenges we put before ourselves, we return to "fight the battle" of everyday life. The barriers and difficulties we confront there can seem so paltry in comparison as we recall our "past labours." We can picture ourselves similarly overcoming our everyday battles.

We are well prepared for life's daily tests, because we know ourselves so much better than had we not confronted the "superiority of fixed purposes, or the perseverance of brute force."

About the Author

 Jack LeMenager is an independent organizational communications consultant with more than twenty-five years of experience in employee communications and business-to-business marketing communications for some of the world's leading companies. His clients have included businesses in industries like consumer goods, insurance, aviation, automotive, medical devices and equipment, pharmaceuticals, chemicals, paper, professional services, and others.

He is the author of the companion book to this volume, "Sandcastles in the Tide: The Value of Employee Communications in the Context of Constant Change."

A California native (Santa Rosa), he earned his Bachelor of Arts degree at Willamette University, Salem, OR, including a year abroad at the University of London (Birkbeck). He spent his early career as a newspaper reporter and editor in Connecticut.

He and his wife, Carolyn, reside in Winchester, MA.

He welcomes your thoughts, comments or questions on this book, as well as any related topics. Please feel free to drop an email to: j.lemenager@comcast.net.

Made in the USA
San Bernardino, CA
24 February 2019